A PORTRAIT OF THE ARTIST

Kennikat Press
National University Publications
Literary Criticism Series

General Editor
John E. Becker

A PORTRAIT OF
THE ARTIST

THE PLAYS OF
TENNESSEE WILLIAMS

FOSTER HIRSCH

National University Publications
KENNIKAT PRESS // 1979
Port Washington, N.Y. // London

Manufactured in the United States of America

Published by
Kennikat Press Corp.
Port Washington, N.Y. / London

Library of Congress Cataloging in Publication Data

Hirsch, Foster.
    A portrait of the artist.

    (National university publications)
    Bibliography: p.
    Includes index.
    1. Williams, Tennessee, 1911– –Criticism and
interpretation. I. Title.
PS3545.I5365Z68   812'.5'4   78-26480
ISBN 0-8046-9230-0

CONTENTS

ABOUT THE AUTHOR

Foster Hirsch is Associate Professor of English and Film at Brooklyn College. He has written numerous articles for the *New York Times,* the *Nation, The New Republic* and many other publications. He is also the author of several books on film and literature, including studies of Edward Albee, George Kelly, Laurence Olivier, and the Epic Film.

A PORTRAIT OF THE ARTIST

1

THE MAN AND HIS WORK

Nymphomania, promiscuity, rape, greed, alcoholism, impotence, homosexuality, profligacy, frigidity, crib fetishism, pedophilia, blowtorch killing, castration, dope addiction, venereal disease, cannibalism, madness, panty fetishism, masturbation, coprophagy: gleefully listed by *Playboy*,[1] these are the subjects that have preoccupied Tennessee Williams, our national poet of the perverse, "the man whom we pay to have our nightmares for us."[2] Drawing on his own erotic fantasies, shocking and charming audiences with his hothouse visions of sex and violence, Tennessee Williams is a popular entertainer who is at the same time a serious artist.

With his poet's sense of rhythm and image, Williams embellishes his dramas with elaborate symbols. The glass menagerie, the streetcar named Desire, the rose tattoo, the *camino real*, the Venus fly trap in *Suddenly Last Summer*, the cavern in *Period of Adjustment*, the iguana in *The Night of the Iguana*, the clipped flowers in *In the Bar of a Tokyo Hotel*, are all bluntly insisted-upon signs and tokens of Williams's serious literary purpose. "My great bête noir as a writer," Williams has admitted, in the face of some hard criticism, "has been a tendency . . . to poeticize."[3]

In his early and middle periods—his great creative streak from *The Glass Menagerie* in 1945 to *The Night of the Iguana* in 1961—Williams was writing to reach a mass audience. "I feel it can dig what I have to say, perhaps better than a lot of intellectuals can . . . the bigger the audience, the better."[4] Always wanting to please—"I have a great desire to *excite* people!"—Williams was at the same time anxious to write well, to deepen theme and characterization with a carefully worked out pattern of symbols.

3

Williams has always tried to write emotionally complex plays in which he placed his characters within a cosmic frame. To that end, sex is never simply sex in a Williams drama: in *Suddenly Last Summer,* for instance, Sebastian Venable's sexual appetite symbolizes cosmic rapacity; his greed, his urge to devour, is but the echo of God's relation to man. In *A Streetcar Named Desire* Stanley Kowalski's seduction of Blanche Du Bois is not merely the victory of a hard-hat over a coy Southern belle, it is the representation of Williams's conviction that the meek shall *not* inherit the earth. The battle over the farm in *Kingdom of Earth* is not only a contest between two types of male sexuality, it is a symbolic struggle for possession of the South. Val Xavier, the hero of *Battle of Angels* and *Orpheus Descending,* is not simply a stud who infuriates a backwater Southern town, he is the savior who revitalizes every woman he meets. All of Williams's muscular heroes, in fact, from Val Xavier to Chance Wayne in *Sweet Bird of Youth* to Chris Flanders in *The Milk Train Doesn't Stop Here Any More,* are angels of mercy whose bodies are the instruments of resurrection and purification.

Although they often contain sensational elements, Williams's plays are as moralistic as they are literary. "Tom is not a dirty writer," his brother Dakin has insisted. "He is really turning out morality plays. . . . He is searching for pardon for the sinner in the mercy of an all-loving God."[5] The plays are a series of moral allegories in which Williams, an entrenched puritan fascinated by his own and others' sinfulness, judges his characters. He is a moralist who exposes corruption: "I think that deliberate, conscienceless mendacity, the acceptance of falsehood and hypocrisy is the most dangerous of all sins. The moral contribution of my plays is that they uncover what I consider to be untrue."[6] Williams's characters are thus examples of various roads to ruin and the consequences of sin. Since Williams has never shaken the notion that sex is at least partly sinful, all of his sexually troubled characters are held to a strict moral reckoning; and their unhappy histories are designed as warnings. Williams concocts exotic sexual fantasies, yet he hovers puritanically over the revels, seeing to it that the misbehaving characters are properly punished. Though Williams believes that sex is a form of grace, he also feels that sex is impure, and he often resolves his contradictory attitudes by contriving horrible destinies for his sexual athletes. Williams is a confused moralist, and his continuing battle with his puritanical impulses frequently complicates the dramas in interesting ways. The plays are filled with tantalizing ambiguities.

Williams creates driven characters who are unlike anyone most of us are ever likely to meet and yet they are almost all convincing and recognizable. Williams's special gift is exactly his ability to give universal dimension to his private fantasy figures. In his successful period, from 1945 to 1961, his plays appealed to millions, from matinee matrons to *The Partisan Review*, from adolescents to English professors. Different kinds of audiences were titillated, challenged, and absorbed by Williams's original vision. After enjoying long runs in New York, most of the plays had lengthy national tours before being made into popular movies. In his prime Tennessee Williams was an eminently commercial man of letters.

After *The Night of the Iguana*, though, the writer who converted private trauma into dramatic fireworks lost most of his audience. Williams's personal obsessions derailed him and the plays—from *The Milk Train Doesn't Stop Here* in 1963 to *Out Cry* in 1973—failed to communicate to most theatergoers. The pre-eminent popular playwright of the fifties became the coterie dramatist of the sixties and early seventies. Theatrical and engaging plays like *Cat on a Hot Tin Roof* and *Sweet Bird of Youth* gave way to small-scaled, experimental chamber plays like *Gnadiges Fraulein, In the Bar of a Tokyo Hotel, Small-Craft Warnings,* and *Out Cry*. Consumed by his own neuroses, Williams wrote these decidedly unpopular plays as forms of self-analysis, and the exorcism through his art was more important to him than the courting of public favor.

The details of Williams's fall are as well known as those of his spectacular rise. Like Ernest Hemingway, F. Scott Fitzgerald, Norman Mailer, and Truman Capote, Williams is a full-fledged literary celebrity, a household name whose erratic private life is as much the subject of the gossip column as the scholarly essay. Appearing on talk shows and interviewed by the press, Williams is as famous and as notorious as a misbehaving movie star. For the general public, as well as for the playwright himself, the plays and the life are intimately connected. The dramas, in fact, are written in such a way as to compel us to psychoanalyze their author. When *The Two-Character Play* (the original version of *Out Cry*) opened in London, a critic complained that only Williams's analyst would be able to understand it.

We "read" the man through his work, and the identification has been encouraged by Williams himself. Williams has conspired in the making of his own myth. "I suspect it has always been an instinctive thing with me, when being interviewed, to ham it up and be fairly outrageous in order to provide 'good copy.' The reason? A need to convince the world that I do indeed still exist and to make this fact a matter of public interest and amusement."[7]

To many theatergoers, Williams is a contemporary embodiment of the pagan spirit; a sensualist and bohemian, he is considered in the popular mind to be the author of naughty plays and an ornament to café society. In an interview with Williams in *Esquire,* Rex Reed provided a lush description of the playwright as an ultimate voluptuary and aesthete, living in a world that is a "gilt-edged invitation to decadence ... with constantly recurring visions in a madhouse, laced with the beckoning insinuation of champagne and flaming foods, of Oriental rugs and dimly lit brothels, surrounded by exotic friends like Anaïs Nin and Anna Magnani. He has gathered his years slowly, savoring the lusty taste of living, taking swooning delight in extravaganzas of brocade, crepe suzettes, and a mild scent of orrisroot."[8]

In addition to his bohemian style Williams's medical history has always been public information, and the author himself, in interviews, and later in his *Memoirs,* talks compulsively and with a sort of macabre glee, about his series of mental breakdowns, his problems with drugs and alcohol, his heart palpitations, his claustrophobia, his cataracts, his recurrent fears of imminent death, his intense depression over his sister's lobotomy, his suicidal mood after the death of Frank Merlo, the man with whom he had lived for fourteen years. At the lowest point in his personal and professional fortunes, in the late sixties, Williams's confinement to an institution received more attention than his plays.

"To tell the truth," Williams has said, "I'm just too damn self-centered. The problems of my private life occupy too much of my attention."[9] Williams has called himself one of the world's "most egocentric" people; and for him, as for many of the characters in his later plays, life and art mingle incestuously. "At the age of fourteen I discovered writing as an escape from a world of reality in which I felt acutely uncomfortable. . . . [writing was] my place of retreat, my cave, my refuge."[10] Williams even discontinued psychoanalysis because his doctor wanted him "to take a rest" from writing. "He'd shift my appointment hours to try to make it impossible for me to work. But if he said to come in at eight a.m., I'd get up at four and do my writing. I just couldn't face a day without work."[11]

Dramatizing his own fears, his paranoia, his maladjustment to the "real world," his sexual conflicts, his intense guilt, Williams can write only about "things that concern me . . . I just have to identify with the character in some way, or the character is not real. I sometimes wish that my writing was less personal. In recent years I think my outlook became almost like a scream."[12]

Trapped in his own "heart, body and brain, [which] are forged in a white-hot furnace for the purpose of conflict," Williams has been preoccupied in his plays with two consuming themes that are the dominant struggles in his own life: the conflict between the puritan and the cavalier, which absorbs him throughout his early and middle periods, and the artist's relation to art, which has detained him throughout the last decade. The body and the soul, life and art—these great dualities provide the conflicts in both the plays and the life of Tennessee Williams.

Williams inherits from his parents his continuing struggle between the flesh and the spirit. His mother is a rector's daughter descended from Quakers, and his father was a brawny manager of a shoe company who, says Mrs. Williams, "liked long poker games and drinking bouts . . . and would talk in a rough way in front of the children."[13] Mr. Williams uprooted the family, and the move from a rural rectory in Mississippi to a grim city apartment in St. Louis represented for young Tom and his mother a rude cultural shock. Williams was always at war with his father, whose own virility was offended by his son's quiet manner and his interest in books. As Williams has often told interviewers, his father persistently called him sissy and "Miss Nancy." "When I was younger," Williams says, "I hated him with a passionate loathing. He was a big, powerful man, and he intimidated all of us. . . . My mother hated his guts too. She still does. She doesn't have a good word to say for him, and didn't even attend his funeral."[14]

A father who strikes terror in the heart of his son ("he scared me all my life"[15]), a mother who exemplified Southern gentility—here, in his unhappy family history, developed the conflict that appears in Williams's strongest plays. The real life models for hulking, threatening Stanley Kowalski and fluttery Blanche Du Bois were Mr. and Mrs. Williams.

Williams's family heritage is introduced in many of his major plays. Like the playwright himself, his characters are often caught between the world of the rectory and that of Moon Lake Casino, which is the symbol in the early plays of the fast party life to which Williams and characters like Alma Winemiller and Blanche Du Bois are both attracted and repelled. Williams has said that he identifies more with Alma, the divided heroine of *Summer and Smoke,* than with any of his other characters: "Alma is my favorite—because I came out so late and so did Alma, and she had the greatest struggle."[16] Like Alma, Williams grew up in the rarefied atmosphere of a country rectory which both sheltered and stifled him; and like Alma, he left it for something racier—bohemian life in New Orleans. Williams, like the narrator in *The Glass Menagerie*, felt he had to leave his confining family home, but he was never able to escape his moralistic upbringing. Williams rebelled against the genteel tradition in which his mother raised him: "I try to outrage puritanism. I have an instinct to shock."[17] But Williams is an uneasy rebel, since he feels that sex is sinful as well as liberating and since he alternately condemns and worships the life of the body. For Williams, as Marion Magid has written, "normal adult sexuality" is a "catastrophe": "In the end, Williams's vision is revealed as a shocked outcry, a child's refusal to accept the fact of sex that, yes, grownups really do it."[18]

Williams's discomfort with sex underlies most of the plays, and many of his characters are projections of varying parts of his own complicated sexuality. A character like Alma represents with almost diagrammatic simplicity Williams's own split between refinement and rapacity. A character like Serafina (in *The Rose Tattoo*) celebrates Williams's worship of sex, while a character like Blanche indicates his fear of it.

It was not until 1970 that Williams began to speak openly about his homosexuality, and it was not until his interview with *Playboy* in 1973 that he spoke about it without defensiveness. "Until I was twenty-eight, I was attracted to girls," Williams confided to *Playboy*,

Blanches 1st husband

but after that I fell in love with a man and felt it was better for me as a writer, for it meant *freedom*.... Women have always been my deepest emotional root; anyone who's read my writings knows that. But I've never had any feeling of sexual security—except with Frank Merlo, who served me as I had to be served ... my first real encounter was in New Orleans at a New Year's Eve Party during World War Two. A very handsome paratrooper climbed up to my grilled veranda and said, "Come down to my place," and I did, and he said, "Would you like a sunlamp treatment?" and I said, "Fine," and I got under one and he proceeded to do me. That was my coming out and I enjoyed it.[19]

In 1975 Williams published a novel, *Moise and the World of Reason*, and his *Memoirs*, in both of which he continues the sexual confessions begun in the now notorious *Playboy* interview. In the novel and particularly in *Memoirs*, Williams writes openly about homosexuality, in a way that he never felt free to in his great masked plays. The novel reads in fact like a dry run for the revelations in *Memoirs,* though the tone of *Moise* is darker than that of the autobiography, its treatment of sexuality less jubilant: its homosexual love story is an intimation of the expansive confessional mode that explodes full-force in *Memoirs.*

Moise and the World of Reason reads like a series of journal entrees in which the author muses at random on art and sex, his twin preoccupations. The novel's compulsively voluble narrator clearly speaks to us in Williams's own palpitating voice, creating a portrait of the author as a sensual young man, "a distinguished failed writer" at thirty. Obsessed with his past, his sexual desires, and his rejection slips, the narrator uses his diary jottings as a defense against emptiness. His desk (as for Williams) is the center of his world; his writing imposes order and dignity on the experiences of a sometimes shabby life. Art heals, and the book records the process of the writer's salvation through the patterned arrangement of words on a page. Since it has no real story or tangible dramatic conflict, the novel is designed to show off its author's sensibility—Williams attempts to hold us with the fractured, fevered ruminations of a fictional character who nakedly enacts his own fears of artistic failure and isolation. On a long, dark night of the soul, after he has been abandoned at a party by his current lover, the narrator returns to his hovel to scribble and to reflect; and we are regaled with a free-form kaleidoscopic sampling of what is on his mind. Characters, anecdotes, images from Williams's own past compete for our attention. Williams is an exuberant, though inconsistent, master of ceremonies, and the quality of the remembered moments varies. Some are tantalizing, while others seem like pale carbon copies of past routines. A vivid caricature of a voracious woman called the Actress Invicta is presented in Williams's florid, Rabelaisian grand manner; but a scene between the narrator and his conservative Southern mother, who is shocked by her son's bohemian ways, is shrill and mechanical.

As always, Williams is a poet of sexual longing; and the most lyrical of the memories involve the writer and his first lover Lance, a black ice skater with an ideal physique and a generous, yielding spirit. Typically, Williams's attitude to sex is dense and contradictory as he sees it as both holy and infected, transcendent and tainted. Lance is a Williams stud like Stanley Kowalski and Chance Wayne who offers ecstatic release. Yet throughout these reminiscences sex is also sinister, as in the bizarre passage in which the young writer meets and feels threatened by a once-famous playwright who tries to entice him to go on a long journey. The crumbling playwright, so patently an embittered self-portrait, uses sex as magic but also as punishment. An experience that the narrator recalls from childhood also connects sex with doom. The remembered incident concerns the sudden appearance in the author's small Southern hometown of four elegant young men who lure boys into their car; to the narrator, the crusaders seem fatally corrupt, their compulsive, ritualistic cruising a prefiguring of early death.

Williams therefore remains a reluctant Dionysian, a guilt-ridden reveler; and for this Southern puritan, sex still sometimes promises catastrophe. But until this point in his writing, Williams had never before written so unguardedly about himself. The narrator is openly, at times even joyously, homosexual, so that sexual desire isn't disguised here as it was in the plays. Williams, however, is one of those writers for whom telling all may have a therapeutic effect on his spirit but a dampening result on his art. Written before gay liberation, his major plays required distance from and transformation of his actual experience, and Williams benefited, artistically, from the pressures imposed by social convention. (On one level *A Streetcar Named Desire* is a homosexual fantasy with Blanche as an effeminate male masked as a magnificently neurotic Southern belle; but American drama can be grateful that Williams didn't write Blanche as a man!) Except for *Memoirs*, *Moise and the World of Reason* is Williams's most open personal statement, and yet it has little of the surging erotic comedy or the dynamic tensions of the great partially closed plays.

Memoirs is Williams's ultimate coming out statement, and a vigorous reinforcement of the playwright's belief that the work and the life of a writer are inextricably bound. Like all of Williams's writing, these private revelations are obsessively concerned with sex, but here sexuality offers joy and refuge from isolation without the darker aspects of self-punishment and loss of self that often taint sex in the plays. Williams's relationships with men have caused him much pain, but in this wonderfully liberated and liberating book, Williams celebrates the pleasures of loving men. He writes about his homosexuality without apology. There is a serene self-acceptance evident here that represents a marked difference from the tortured, divided, sexually frustrated characters in many of his plays. He seems to have shed the puritanical values that have nagged him for most of his life: at long last, after years in the shadows of his grandfather's rectory, after years of analysis and conflict, Williams seems to be a free spirit, a true, guiltless voluptuary.

Because he wanted to get his plays produced, Williams had to disguise the homosexual motifs that were given free rein in early stories like

"One Arm" and "Hard Candy." Like Proust, Williams felt he had to trans-
pose and readjust the sexual currents in order to reach a large audience.
Because homosexuality was in the forties and fifties an unmentionable
subject, Williams had to transfer to his often grasping, hot-blooded female
characters his own intense attraction to men. What *Memoirs* makes clear
is that, if social attitudes toward homosexuality had been different, his
work would have been different, too. *Memoirs* doesn't change the plays,
but it compels us to admit their masks and transpositions. Many critics
have hinted at the homosexual aura of the plays, pointing out that it is
almost always the men who are the sex objects, the sexual saviors and
magicians. Now the atmosphere of critical innuendo, the veiled charges,
can be dispelled, for Williams has given his critics enough frank details to
liberate them as well as himself.

Williams takes evident delight in startling his readers, referring exhi-
bitionistically to his mental and physical collapses. His section on his
confinement in a violent ward of a mental institution is harrowing, though
written with a kind of impish pride—Williams seems to take a perverse
pleasure in recounting the sensational details of his incarceration, and the
scenes in the hospital are shot through with flashes of grim comedy.
Perhaps it is this sense of life's comedy that has saved Williams. *Memoirs*
reveals his mordant sense of humor, his healing irony in the midst of pain,
his great capacity for laughter. Williams's recent confessional writing,
lively, direct, immediate, nevertheless misses the soaring, lyrical intensity
of his best work. Yet an innocence emanates from these revved-up self-
portraits; there is something, finally, unspoiled about Williams. As revealed
in both the novel and *Memoirs,* his goal of unwavering dedication to his
art and his ambition to be the best writer that he is capable of being,
are altogether admirable. *Memoirs* shows enormous courage. It is a land-
mark in American letters that enriches our understanding of the work
of a great playwright.

Williams didn't have to "come out," of course, for his audience to
know the truth about his sexual preferences, since on one level, almost all
the plays are homosexual fantasies. Williams's women desire spectacular
males, and between the playwright and his ravenous females there is a
deep emotional connection. In *Cat on a Hot Tin Roof,* Maggie pleads for
Brick to go to bed with her; Alma has a schoolgirl's crush on the handsome doctor who lives next door; Blanche is both alarmed by and
attracted to the sight of Stanley's rippling muscles; the women of a provincial Southern town pant after the sultry wanderer, Val Xavier, in

Battle of Angels. In Williams's most exotic fantasy, *Suddenly Last Summer,* Sebastian Venable is eaten alive by a group of native boys; and in his most seemingly heterosexual play, *Period of Adjustment,* the army buddies are more comfortable with each other than with their shrill wives. The virile male, the peacock, the stud, is the central icon in play after play; he is the catalyst, the fought over, the scapegoat, the victim, the prize. Williams worships him, lusts after him, punishes him; the stud's sexuality is both reward and threat. The beautiful, muscled young man is the animate object that ignites the spinsters and the whores. In most of Williams's plays, the man rather than the woman is the desirable partner; and it is women who are sexually aggressive—the men don't have to be. No Williams play is written on the pattern of the traditional heterosexual chase.

The homosexual sensibility is always present, though it is almost never direct, since Williams writes about men with women rather than about men with men. Only in *Small-Craft Warnings* and *Vieux Carre* does Williams present an overtly homosexual relationship, and only in these plays do characters talk openly about the gay life. The homosexual impulse often masquerades as heterosexual courtship. Williams's women, however, must not be interpreted as drag queens. They "play" as women because Williams has transmuted private fantasy into art. There is no simple, easy equation between the playwright and his man-hungry women; rather, Williams has used his own deepest sexual impulses as the base on which to construct complex dramatic characters. His homosexuality necessarily colors the way he presents both his female and male characters; as he has often said, he identifies more with his women than with his men, but this does not mean that Williams's females are merely effeminate men in disguise, or that Williams is cheating by trying to pass off a character like Blanche as a woman. The millions of viewers and readers who have accepted Blanche as a woman have not been duped by a clever dramatist writing plays in code for a coterie audience; but there is much in Blanche's extravagantly stylized personality, in her flirtatiousness, her quivering sensitivity, her concern with surface, that is reflective of certain kinds of gay as well as "straight" female sensibilities. A character like Blanche, created by a homosexual, is a mixture of several different sexual currents. As either gay or straight, she is an outsider, like most of the playwright's characters, a reject from conventional society, and it is this sense of her absolute isolation that Williams creates so powerfully and that "mixed" audiences throughout the world have continued to respond to with great empathy. Though conceived by a writer who felt estranged and who suffered because he was homosexual, Williams's outcasts have significance for audiences beyond gay ghettoes. The universal resonance of his characters has of course been responsible for Williams's high literary reputation. And it is because he has always tried to reach "mixed" audiences that Williams has resisted writing specifically gay plays like *The Boys in the Band*. Except perhaps in *Cat on a Hot Tin Roof*, sexual masking in Williams is not then necessarily hypocritical, and it certainly does not diminish his creative strengths, no more than it does in Proust.

Williams does not write disguised gay liberation tracts that covertly exalt homosexual love. Plays like *Cat on a Hot Tin Roof* and *Period of Adjustment* present heterosexual relationships in an unattractive way, but this derision is never the central focus of Williams's work. The playwright may often exalt the male and humiliate the female, but he identifies always with his victims, and so his sympathy is reserved for his hounded, rejected, dishevelled women rather than his cool, self-absorbed Adonises, upon whom he inflicts appalling punishment: Chance Wayne in *Sweet Bird of Youth* is castrated; Val Xavier in *Battle of Angels* is lynched; Sebastian Venable in *Suddenly Last Summer* is cannibalized.

Ever present, homosexuality in Williams is almost always concealed. In that jittery mid-fifties play, *Cat on a Hot Tin Roof*, it is the disease that dare not speak its name, and it is equated with another dreadful affliction— cancer. When he touches on it directly, Williams frequently presents homosexuality in a grim context. The homosexual in *Small-Craft Warnings*, for instance, derides gay promiscuity; and since he has been corrupted and coarsened by gay experience, he has lost the ability to be surprised by life. In *Suddenly Last Summer* Williams treats gay cruising as the emblem of a rotting universe. Homosexuals in the plays are often stereotypes that confirm popular prejudice: gays in Williams are supremely sensitive artists; aesthetes who are too refined for the world as it is; sybarites compulsively addicted to sex. In *Cat on a Hot Tin Roof*, Brick's friend Skipper kills himself when he realizes that he is homosexual and Brick himself retreats to a kind of death-in-life.

Until *Memoirs*, it was only in Williams's novella, "The Knightly Quest," that the overt homosexual was presented favorably. Gewinner Pierce is a romantic whose refinement is clearly superior to the bestial coupling of his gross heterosexual brother and his crass wife. Gewinner easily triumphs over brutish straights who inhabit a plastic countryside littered with hamburger joints. Together with two sympathetic women, Gewinner is transported in a spaceship to a better world than the rancid contemporary America he judges so harshly.

Williams has said recently that he never considered homosexuality a promising subject for a full-length play, and he has confined direct rather than masked or metaphoric treatments of the subject to short stories. In "Desire and the Black Masseur" a meek man meets his destiny being pummeled to death by a towering black masseur: the story is a fantasy confrontation between the ultimate masochist and the ultimate sadist. In "One Arm" the hustler protagonist services men rather than women. "Mysteries of the Joy Rio" and "Hard Candy" are two versions of the same subject, fleeting sex in the balcony of a fading movie palace. An old man finds pleasure with a series of compliant, anonymous, sometimes faceless young men and boys. The homosexual life patterns described in these stories are not presented from a liberated or crusading viewpoint. Sex in these explicit stories is dank and joyless, even if the stories end, curiously, with a kind of catharsis: unhappy sex is linked to death and a final mystical transfiguration. The characters are all sinners who are yet saved by compulsive, serial sex; impersonal sex leads to salvation, and the characters, who think of themselves as dirty and unworthy, are ultimately purified.

Mixing sex, death, and salvation in beguiling contradiction, Williams is something of a Southern Gothic version of Jean Genet. He is a guilty sex-singer, an unliberated bohemian, a hip puritan who nourishes his art with his own tangled sexual preoccupations. Much has been written about his indebtedness to D. H. Lawrence, and there are certainly connections to Genet in his plays, but Williams is the poet of his own private universe. Williams has claimed "an identification with Lawrence's view of life . . . a belief in the purity of the sensual life,"[20] but he is in fact a much more troubled sensualist than Lawrence. As Nancy Tischler has written, Williams is "not at home in the glorification of sex."[21] Like many of his characters, the playwright wants to escape from the burdens of the flesh, and the horror that taunts him is that the flesh may be an inadequate means to deliverance and transcendence.

Lawrence, Genet, Strindberg, Lorca, Hart Crane, Chekhov, and Ibsen have been proposed at various times as principal influences on Williams. *Time* nominated Hawthorne, Poe, and Melville, "the triumvirate of American gloom and disquietude," as Williams's philosophical forebears: "With them, Williams shares transcendental yearnings, the sense of isolation and alienation, the Calvinist conscience, the Gothic settings and horror."[22] But the only tangible influence on Williams's work has been the effects on him of his family, his friends, and his artistic and commercial fortunes:

his warring parents; his genteel grandparents; his sister Rose, victim of a prefrontal lobotomy for which Williams feels partly responsible; his pliant lover, of fourteen years, Frank Merlo; his identification with wounded people like Diana Barrymore and Carson McCullers and with exuberant voluptuaries like Anna Magnani; his breakdowns and confinements, his withdrawals and resurrections; his resounding critical and popular acceptance, his stunning critical and public rejection.

Williams does, however, belong to a tradition in American letters, that of Southern Gothic, and his settings, his themes, his use of language, share similarities with the work of writers like William Faulkner, Carson McCullers, Jane Bowles, Truman Capote, and Flannery O'Connor. Williams has described what are for him the characteristics that link these Southern writers:

> There is something in the region, something in the blood and culture, of the Southern state that has made [Southerners] the center of this Gothic school of writing. . . . What is this common link? a sense, an intuition, of an underlying dreadfulness in modern experience. . . . The true sense of dread is not a reaction to anything sensible or visible or even, strictly materially, *knowable*. But rather it's a kind of spiritual intuition of something almost too incredible and shocking to talk about, which underlies the whole so-called thing. It is the incommunicable something that we shall have to call *mystery* which is so inspiring of dread . . . that Sense of the Awful which is the desperate black root of nearly all significant modern art.[23]

Like other writers of Southern Gothic, Williams is obsessed with the social outsider, the character who is unbalanced in extravagant and colorful ways. Edged with sexual hysteria, the work of the Gothic writers is intensely theatrical, lushly composed. Their work has a steamy texture, with language and characterization approaching ecstatic overstatement, even when, as in McCullers and O'Connor, there is a serious attempt to write in a cryptic and spare manner. Like other writers in this tradition Williams dramatizes Southern society and the history that hovers prominently behind it as, on the one hand, a malevolent, devouring force and, on the other, an intensely romantic, almost fantasy-like landscape, dotted with white-pillared plantations, weeping willows, and magnolia blossoms. In common with other Southern writers, Williams is absorbed by a romantic vision of the past—the Old South. In many of the plays (and most prominently in *A Streetcar Named Desire* and *The Glass Menagerie*) the characters cling to an idealized notion of plantation society. The picture of an elegant, enclosed society of fine gentlemen courting tremulous ladies in crinoline, while devoted family servants move discreetly in the background, comprises for many of Williams's characters an image of perfect social order. The decline of this rural ideal, as well as the characters' separation from their privileged Southern inheritance, is a measure of their fall from grace, their expulsion from Eden as conceived by the Southern imagination.

Williams's use of Southern history and Southern myth is thus highly sentimental and "aesthetic." In a recent study of the Southern "Renaissance," *The Literature of Memory: Modern Writers of the American South*, Richard Gray evaluates Williams's treatment of Southern motifs as

decorative: it offers us a group of charming grotesques, preserved in amber. What is Southern about it, really, is not a certain quality of perception, a sense of engagement between past and present, the public and the private, myth and history: but a turn of phrase or personality, a use of the bizarre and sensational for their own sake, which has the net effect of creating distance. For regionalism is substituted a form of local color, and a very precious and slightly decadent form at that, in which the gap between drama and audience seems deliberately widened so that the latter can revel without compunction in a contemporary "Gothick" fantasy.[24]

Even if, as Gray suggests, Williams's vision of the South is "decadent" and "reductive," the playwright is nonetheless a distinctly regional writer, and it is perhaps as a popularizer of Southern sensuality and gentility—Southern manners—that he is best known. A major influence on Williams as a creative artist has been precisely his attraction to Southern "style"—to that world of languor and refinement and sensual indulgence which for him are synonymous with the antebellum South. Brass beds, overhead fans, family mansions, suffocating heat, tropical plants—these aspects of the Southern scene permeate the plays, giving the dramas the exotic texture and lush sense of place for which they are famous.

Williams, then, is distinctly a regional writer, steeped in the Southern writer's absorption with the past. The workings of memory, and the collision between a dream of the past and the realities of an increasingly urbanized present provide inspiration for the plays as much as they do for the novels of Faulkner. Williams is writing in the tradition of the Southern "Renaissance," that explosion of literary genius in the twenties as a response to the World War and to the increasing separation of the South from its proudly remembered heritage; and in his tone and sensibility, in his lyricism and dependence on rhetoric, he has more in common with Faulkner and Thomas Wolfe, with Robert Penn Warren and Allen Tate and John Crowe Ransom, than with any tradition in American drama.

Williams, in fact, has exerted far more influence on American drama than he has absorbed from it. His dissection of sexual conflicts anticipated the greater sexual frankness in the plays as well as the films of the sixties and seventies. There is, however, no "school of Williams"—no major writer, or group of writers, has emerged who can claim Williams as a primary inspiration. Williams has remained aloof from trends in American drama, continuing to create plays out of the same basic neurotic conflicts in his own personality. Williams has continued, that is, to borrow from and to be influenced by his own work; as critics of the later plays have only too frequently observed, Williams, heedless of external influences, plagiarizes from himself. The later Williams is still nourished by the distinctive dramatic world created in the earliest plays. That world was so spectacularly scaled and intensely realized that Williams's persistent use of it has come to seem like self-parody. In a sense the playwright has been a victim of his own immediately recognizable style.

Tennessee Williams is a great American original whose work does not reflect his times in any direct way. His plays, though, contain social implications insofar as they are a barometer of what Americans will tolerate or respond to in the way of sexual fantasy and insofar as their acceptance by the public tells us something about the public: "A culture does not consistently pay the price of admission to witness a fable which does not ensnare some part of the truth about it," as Marion Magid noted.[25] But Williams is not interested in being a recorder of public attitudes or social concerns; being among the most private and self-enclosed of famous authors, he writes in order to exorcise his own demons, and he is always triumphantly and inescapably himself.

2

THE BATTLE OF ANGELS
PURITANS AND CAVALIERS

When *Battle of Angels* was presented in Boston on a chilly evening near the end of 1940, it was a colossal failure. Newspaper reviewers were outraged: "The play gives the audience the sensation of having been dunked in mire," proclaimed *The Boston Globe;* "there never was a play crammed with more disagreeable characters."[1] *Variety* complained that "The Theatre Guild may have heard that somebody struck gold down the old tobacco road and decided to dig up a little dirt down along the Mississippi Delta to see how it would pan out."[2] Williams's producers sent a note of apology to subscribers.

An exuberant, passionate play, *Battle of Angels* still has the power to shock audiences. As quirky and out of control as its characters, the play contains evidence of a vigorous original style and a flamboyant theatrical imagination.

Williams was shattered by the hostile reception. He had only written a play, and yet he was treated by crusty Bostonians as if he had committed an indecent public act: "I grew ten years older in one day—for years since I have been disillusioned regarding people."[3] When *The Glass Menagerie* earned him his first success, Williams looked back wistfully at his failure: "That play was, of course, a much better play than this one. The thing is, you can't mix up sex and religion ... but you can always write about mothers."[4]

Williams believed in *Battle of Angels*—"this play is something I wrote directly from my heart as an expression of fundamental human hungers and I felt so intensely that I did not see how it could fail to communicate some feeling to others"[5] —and he returned to it, off and on, for the next seventeen years. He kept at this early play between and even sometimes during the times he was fashioning some of the most popular dramas in the American theatre, and the materials of *Battle of Angels* inevitably influenced *A Streetcar Named Desire, The Rose Tattoo, Summer and Smoke,* and *Cat on a Hot Tin Roof. Battle of Angels* is the root Williams play, a powerful mixture of sex, violence, and religion. A sensual young man; ravenous, deprived matrons; and a backwater town are the play's ingredients. Women want Val Xavier, the play's wandering hero; men resent him. Roving the waterfronts, carousing in bars, enjoying promiscuous sex, Val has been on a continuous "party," and now he wants a more serious life: "I took to moving around. I thought I might track it down, whatever it was I was after. It always kept one jump ahead of me." As Val travels, he writes, trying to create out of his drifter's life the materials for a major philosophical statement: "When people read it, they're going to be frightened. They'll say it's crazy because it tells the truth."

Val has the misfortune to pass through a wildly reactionary Southern community; and since he is a moody, mysterious outsider, a stranger, he disturbs the whole town. Three women are quickly infatuated with him while the sheriff and his henchmen mark him as a deadly adversary. The community, in short, responds to Val in the same way that the first Boston audience responded to the play: as something too hot to handle.

Myra Torrance, Cassandra Whiteside, and Vee Talbot are the play's voracious females for whom the handsome intruder seems heaven-sent. Myra is shackled to a dying, malevolent husband. Cassandra is the town tramp. Vee is possessed by religious visions which she transcribes to canvas. One after the other, and each in her own way, the women attempt to seduce the brooding stranger.

Cassandra sees in Val a fellow spirit, someone with whom to go out drinking and dancing. "You—savage. And me—aristocrat," she suggests. "Both of us things whose license has been revoked in the civilized world. Both of us equally damned and for the same good reason. Because we both want freedom." Although too much alcohol and too much sex have ruined Cassandra, she sees in Val a chance once again to "run wild in the country." Momentarily enticed by the Shavian Life Force that Cassandra embodies, Val capitulates. Cassandra's victory is short-lived, however, for Val has gone beyond the kind of dissipation she offers him.

Because she is a sensible businesswoman, Myra is more appealing to the reformed wanderer. A job in a mercantile store is more tempting for Val than nights in a bar. Myra is the first of Williams's fading but not altogether faded matrons, and her affair with Val is the first treatment of Williams's favorite theme of the rejuvenation of the mature female by the potent young male. Distrustful at first, edgy, afraid of her aroused feelings, Myra finally allows Val into her bedroom. When she bears Val's child, she feels she has been reborn; she is a sleeping princess awakened by a questing knight. Jilted when she was a young, life-loving woman, Myra aborted her child and married a dour older man. She has believed throughout her loveless marriage, though, that her time was not up:

. . . my flesh always crawled when he touched me. Yes, but I stood it . . . I guess I knew in my heart that it wouldn't go on forever, the way I suppose the fig tree knew in spite of those ten useless sprigs it wouldn't be barren always. When you came in off the road and asked for a job, I said to myself, "This is it, this is what you have been waiting for, Myra!" So I said with my eyes, "Stay here, stay here, for the love of God, stay here!" And you did, you stayed. And just about at that time, as though for that special purpose, he started dying upstairs, when I started coming to life.

Myra holds on to Val like a woman possessed. She is even prepared to accuse him of robbing her store if that is the only way she can keep him from leaving her.

Vee Talbot's hysterical reaction to Val leads to the violent climax. Vee, the first of Williams's crazed artists, struggling to paint a vision of Christ, has been unable to complete her picture until she was inspired by Val's handsomeness. Her painting of Val as Christ, however, seems as indecent to her sheriff-husband and his cronies as it did to the original Boston audience, and the town's representatives of the law lynch the intruder.

Battle of Angels dramatizes different kinds of sexual encounters that reappear in many later plays. Sex is seen in the play as both quick and impersonal and as a life-giving force. The notions of sex as promiscuous release and as religious ecstasy violate community convention; and the community retaliates with a brutality that is to be inflicted again and again on Williams's sex offenders. Myra, an adulteress, is shot by her outraged husband; Val, the saintly hustler, is lynched; Vee, who confuses sex and religion, goes mad; and Cassandra, who uses sex as a kind of fix, drowns herself.

Williams has complicated feelings about his transgressors. He always celebrates physical beauty and sexual prowess, and so he is as attracted to Val as his three overwrought female characters are; yet he is compelled to punish his sexual stars. At the time he wrote the play, Williams was hardly better equipped than Sheriff Talbot and his wrathful, envious henchmen to deal with Val.

In play after play Williams first idolizes and then destroys his passionate or passion-arousing young men. Williams cannot allow Val to continue as an angel of mercy who offers his body as earthly solace for lonely women because, at one level, Williams is as horrified as the people in his backwoods town. Tantalized by the notion of the male body as a means of salvation, Williams is also unsettled by the idea, and in giving his savior a ghastly finish, he is satisfying his own moral code; he is punishing his character for having strayed from the community norm. Williams, like his frustrated Southern townspeople, is ultimately threatened by Val's free sensuality, and he uses the lynching as a necessary containment of the hero's Dionysian power.

But Val's violent death is not convincing. "And since his destiny never assumes the rhythm of inevitability," wrote Richard Hayes in *Commonweal,* expressing a common dissatisfaction with the play, "the handing of him over to death ... [is] a wanton stroke, an outrage to human feeling."[6] Williams admits that he had "the greatest trouble with the end of it.... It is so violent and brutal and involved, and could easily get out of hand."[7]

Despite his moral reservations about Val, Williams regards his character as special. He inscribed the play to D. H. Lawrence because in it he had tried "to represent ... one of Lawrence's main ideas which is the almost religious purity and beauty of the sexual relationship." Williams realized, though, that the play's statement is not so simple: "Somehow or other an effect almost the opposite ... seemed to be created in the minds of some of its beholders. ... The idea I meant to convey was perhaps better stated in four lines of a poem that I wrote about the same time:

> Purity and passion are
> things that differ but in name
> and as one metal must emerge
> when melted in a single flame.[8]

Williams certainly wants to believe in the oneness of purity and passion, but he cannot; and his attempt to resolve this conflict is one of the main concerns of his work.

The playwright, then, exalts his wanderer even as he punishes and partially condemns him. He places Val's story within a consciously myth-making frame. The play opens a year after the night of Myra's death and Val's lynching; Myra's store, and the principal artifacts involved in Val's history—his guitar, his snakeskin jacket—are on display, have in fact become a museum that commemorates The Passion of Val and Myra. Two old maid gossips are the museum keepers, and they are assisted by a flamboyantly dressed black shaman, who beckons the spirit of the bohemian voyager. By this framing device, Williams places us in the position of tourists at a sideshow: he wants to shock us.

Orpheus Descending (1957) is the second, and more mature, version of Val's story. Williams lived with the character for a long time, and when he finally finished with him, he aged him from twenty-five to thirty and sub-mitted him to a general chastening. The second Val also feels the pressure of time, and even more than the earlier character he wants to retreat into a kind of bodiless limbo. He wants to be free of the world in which people are "bought and sold . . . like carcasses of hogs in butcher shops." His image of freedom is

a kind of bird that don't have legs so it can't light on nothing but has to stay all its life on its wings in the sky. . . . You can't tell those birds from the sky and that's why the hawks don't catch them. . . . They sleep on the wind and . . . never light on this earth but one time when they die! . . . I'd like to be one of those birds; they's lots of people would like to be one of those birds and never be—corrupted!

Val is one of the playwright's cerebral sensualists, cool and almost puritanical. Though he is a reluctant lover, this more subdued Val still attracts women. Myra (renamed Lady) still moves him into her downstairs alcove. Cassandra (renamed Carol) sees in him the unmistakable markings of the fugitive kind. And Vee still confuses him with the Savior.

Val is a musician instead of a writer in this revised version. His guitar serves as the play's obsessive phallic symbol, but it is used also, like the book in the earlier play, as a symbol of Val's salvation through art. The guitar is his "life's companion! It washes me clean like water when any-thing unclean has touched me." Warm-blooded ("my temperature's always a few degrees above normal, the same as a dog's"), purity-seeking despite his party life, Val is a loner. In a famous speech, he says that everyone is confined, from birth, in his own skin: "Nobody ever gets to know *no body!* We're all of us sentenced to solitary confinement inside our skins, for life! . . . we're under a life-long sentence to solitary confinement inside our own lonely skins for as long as we live on this earth!"

This mellow, ethereal Adonis is still a threat to the narrow Southern community, however, and the play ends with Val's lynching. Although the finale is less melodramatic than in *Battle of Angels*, it still does not seem convincing.

Lady has been given a fuller history in this second version of the material. Her father ran a kind of restaurant-brothel which was burned because the townspeople were enraged that the establishment sold liquor to a black man. The destruction of the winegarden prefigures the town's destruction of Val. The excited recital of Lady's family background replaces the museum framework of the earlier play.

Val in this later drama is not only a Christ figure, one who has healing powers and one who is crucified by a mob that cannot and does not want to understand him, but a figure of pagan myth as well—Orpheus descending to the Underworld. Despite the added symbolism, this is a more controlled treatment of the same theme, the basic theme, in fact, of Williams's work.

Based on two short stories by D. H. Lawrence and written with his good friend Donald Windham, *You Touched Me* (1946) is Williams's only collaborative effort. A very early play, completed before *The Glass Menagerie,* it is a rough draft for Williams's great recurrent theme: the contrast between the open world of sexual pleasure and the closed world of sexual denial. In this simplistic novice play Williams pits puritan against cavalier and uncharacteristically grants the latter a clear-cut triumph.

In its bald separation between those who enjoy the pleasures of the flesh and those who do not, the play is a forerunner of two other forties plays, *Summer and Smoke* and *A Streetcar Named Desire;* the former is only slightly more sophisticated in its judgments than *You Touched Me,* and the latter is Williams's most complex and powerful statement on the contrasts between puritans and cavaliers.

The three plays (which form more of a group than critical recognition has indicated) are alike in setting up a delicate female and a sexually expressive male for moral evaluation. Hadrian in *You Touched Me,* Dr. John Buchanan in *Summer and Smoke,* and Stanley Kowalski in *A Streetcar Named Desire* are exponents of the open, cavalier life who have terrific impact on inhibited women. Matilda, the heroine of *You Touched Me,* is severely though not hopelessly repressed by her rigid, sex-fearing aunt. Alma Winemiller is a minister's daughter heading toward spinster-hood. Blanche Du Bois, the most guilt-ridden of these early Williams neurotics who need so much to be saved, has the manner of a genteel aristocrat and the habits of a prostitute.

The heroes of the three plays are the liberating princes. Hadrian rescues Matilda; Dr. John Buchanan's high spirits push Alma to attempt a very different kind of life from the one she has known in the rectory; Stanley Kowalski causes Blanche to collapse, and her breakdown releases her from the burdens of living a double life. Of these three male instigators, Hadrian is the most innocent and pallid, and significantly, he is the most success-ful. Williams gives the character a grand entrance: when Hadrian strides into Matilda's musty, dainty parlor, "the sun emerges. The smoke from the engine which is directly across the road puffs into the open door about his figure and the mist has a yellowish glow." Hadrian is both animal and saint, "a clean-cut, muscular young man in the dress uniform of a lieutenant in the Royal Canadian Air Force" with "something about him which the unsympathetic might call sharp or fox-like. It is a look, certainly, that might be observed in the face of a young animal of the woods who has preserved his life through tense exercise of a physical craft and quickness." But "behind that quickness is something else—a need, a sensitivity, a sad patient waiting for something."

On leave from the Air Force, Hadrian returns to the home of his adopted father Captain Rockley, who is dominated by his prim, iron-willed sister Emmie. Hadrian is the intruding angel, the bringer of light to Emmie's dark parlor. Polemicist, radical, orator, he has returned home fired by ideas of openness:

Now the war's over—we've got to explore new countries of the mind, and colonize them. Not just a Columbus or two, but whole great boat-loads of fearless colonists have to set foot in those countries and make homes there—not prefabricated—but on a vast and everlasting-scale! And there mustn't be any peace, but a new war's beginning. . . . The war for life, not against. The war to create a world that can live without war. All the dead bodies of Europe, all of the corpses of Africa, Asia, America ought to be raised on flagpoles over the world, and the cities not built up but left as they are—a shambles, a black museum—. . . to stroll about in—on Sunday afternoons—in case you forget—and leave the world to chance, and the rats of advantage.

Hadrian, an apostle of change and expansion, is exactly the sort of vigorous man Matilda needs to wrench her away from her aunt's sterile parlor.

Unlike Alma or Blanche, Matilda escapes; but then she is far less hysterical than the others. She is merely a giddy schoolgirl who overreacts to Hadrian's touch when, in the dark, she lightly embraces him, believing she is comforting her father. (Williams said the play dramatizes "the almost metaphysical power of the touch."[9]) When she discovers that it is Hadrian rather than her father who is returning her touch, she is extremely troubled. But she is "cured" because her sexual maladjustments are only superficial—she is innocent, not insane.

You Touched Me was advertised as a romantic comedy; and technically, since it has a conventional happy ending, it is. The authors try to keep the tone light, treating the interfering characters, Aunt Emmie and her priggish suitor, the rector, as comic opera buffoons. It is because she is so foolish that Aunt Emmie is not, finally, a formidable antagonist to the crusading Hadrian.

A simplistic early version of Williams's favorite theme, *You Touched Me* is marred not only by its farcical treatment of the puritans and its uneasy blend of broad comedy and conventional romance, but also by its unconvincing social consciousness. Hadrian's message of social progress is strained. Joseph Wood Krutch noted the play's awkward mixture of sex and politics; the worst scenes, he wrote, "are those in which the attempt is made to give this personal drama some significance both political and cosmic. . . . There may be some connection between phallic worship and a new league of nations, but it is not to me immediately a very clear one."[10]

The play is more typical of Williams in its heavy-handed use of symbols. Williams borrows the image of the fox in the chicken coop from Lawrence's story "The Fox": man-hating Aunt Emmie is intent on removing the fox both inside and outside her parlor. And Williams also uses the deserted pottery house that is attached to the Captain's cottage for symbolic heightening; the dim, empty space represents the closed life from which Matilda must free herself.

The play, then, pivots the open and the closed approaches to life; it contrasts the puritan with the cavalier, the liberated with the enchained, in an altogether naive way not to appear again in Williams's writing. The drama is a direct plea for "Life and Growth amid all this destruction and disintegration" (a quotation from Lawrence that appeared in the New York playbill). Aware of the play's message-mongering, Williams apologized:

It is an allegory nearly as moral as an Aesop's fable, but I hope that the allegory is not too obtrusive. If you prefer to overlook it, you may see only the simple love story which it is built on.... It could have been didactic. It was our job to keep it light and moving, to give it full value as entertainment.[11]

With its two fresh young lovers and its happy ending, the play does please in superficial ways. It is an undemanding Broadway comedy that nonetheless contains intimations of the deeper, darker works to come. Not for once working on his own, Williams's voice is muted, and the critic for *The Catholic World* noted that *You Touched Me* is "a music box which plays four different tunes ... Henry Arthur Jones, Chekhov, O'Neill, Ibsen-Lawrence."[12] Aside from the insistent symbolism, the play's one unmistakably Williams touch is the characterization of Captain Rockley. Like many later Williams characters, he is in decline. Having lost command of his ship, and sinking into an alcoholic stupor, the Captain is nonetheless a much livelier opponent than Hadrian to the world of the abandoned pottery house; with his ribald jokes, blatant virility, and full-bodied laugh, he is a forerunner of Big Daddy in *Cat on a Hot Tin Roof*. Although Williams has said that he doesn't like this kind of character, his towering father figures are always vivid. Captain Rockley is a more persuasively written character than Hadrian, and this is fatal to the play's theme.

Compared to moody Val Xavier or Stanley Kowalski or even to Dr. John Buchanan, Hadrian is an unconvincing Adonis. It is significant, though, that this least threatening and least seductive of Williams's muscular protagonists is also the most successful—he wins his girl and conquers his adversaries. When Williams creates a truly intimidating character, like Stanley or Val, he is almost as uncomfortable with him as his convention-bound characters are. But Hadrian, with his ideals about world unity and his search for a mother figure, is not much of a threat to anyone except prim fools like Aunt Emmie.

Dull, cardboard Hadrian fails the play in the same way that Dr. John Buchanan's vacuity undermines *Summer and Smoke*. More than most critics have realized, it is Williams's male catalysts rather than his flamboyant female neurotics who give shape to the plays. When the males are vividly, even if ambivalently, dramatized—Stanley Kowalski is the pre-eminent example—the plays have emotional complexity. But when Williams's heroes are as thinly conceived as Hadrian and John Buchanan, the inevitable sexual battle is diminished.

In *Summer and Smoke* once again a high-spirited, sensual young man changes the life of a repressed young woman. But here, working on his own and freed from the problems of adaptation, Williams regards his characters from a more complicated perspective than in *You Touched Me,* and *Summer and Smoke* is not so obvious an affirmation of the open life.

The play shares with *Battle of Angels* Williams's typically ambivalent reaction to the sex-singer. The hero changes radically in the course of the action. At first he is robust and gregarious, and the minister's daughter is infatuated with him because he represents for her the bohemian life from which she is excluded by background and temperament. Williams acknowledges his hero's appeal, but he also disapproves of him, and the action of the play is designed to "correct" his carefree hero. Dr. John leaves town after his father is killed by the father of the Mexican girl he is planning to marry; and when he returns years later, he has reformed. He becomes engaged to a respectable local girl and he devotes himself to his work.

Ironically, John's reformation releases Alma, and in the enigmatic last scene, she is very different from the breathless, high-strung eccentric of act 1. Much too patly, the two characters change places. John is Flesh turned Spirit; Alma, Spirit transformed to Flesh. They are stick figures in a morality drama. For John, in the beginning of the play, life is the satisfaction of physical appetites; for Alma it is "the everlasting struggle and aspiration for more than our human limits have placed in our reach." John teaches Alma by showing her an anatomy chart while Alma's lesson to John is based on Gothic cathedrals—"the immense stained windows, the great arched doors that are five or six times the height of the tallest man—the vaulted ceiling and the delicate spires—all reaching up to something beyond attainment!"

John is cynical, but he is attractive. Alma is noble and earnest, but she is dowdy. The two of them circle each other in a wary courtship dance (John says, "I'm more afraid of your soul than you're afraid of my body"). Ultimately they exchange allegiances, with John becoming a respected member of the community and Alma entering a bohemian life.

Williams regards John with detachment, and he makes neither his sexuality nor his later sobriety very credible. Williams is very interested in Alma, however; he has said repeatedly, in fact, that Alma is his favorite character: "I think the character I like most is Miss Alma. . . . She really had the greatest struggle. . . . You see, Alma went through the same thing

I went through—from puritanical shackles to, well, complete p
. . . Freedom. Liberation from taboos."[13]

Alma is the first full-scale treatment of the most famous
archetype, the flighty, sexually frustrated, eccentric matron. Alr
manner encourages people to laugh at her. She is affected and ela
genteel. Excluded from normal society, she has formed a cultura
consisting of people who are as unaccepted as she is. Williams
Alma's circle with both sympathy and derision. We are supposed t
at these spinsters and effeminate men, these loners and rejects, but
also clearly supposed to feel sorry for them: the scene of their cu
meeting expresses Williams's deep identification with social outs

Williams is perhaps transferring to his mocked and ostracized heroine
the kind of humiliation he suffered himself as a "Miss Nancy" who pre-
ferred to read rather than to play ball with the neighborhood kids. Suffering the consequences of a rigid, puritanical upbringing, Alma, like Williams,
idealizes the body and moves from longing for the bohemian life to actual
participation in it. At the end of the play, she propositions a traveling
salesman, their meeting place to be the notorious Moon Lake Casino.
For Alma, a night at the Casino realizes all her fantasies of sinfulness.
Williams believes that people contain intense sexual contradictions and so
Alma is capable of being both a spinster and a prostitute just as Val Xavier
is a hustler who seeks purity.

Critics accused Williams of writing a schematic play in which the
doctor's wild son and the minister's genteel daughter exchange places.
The play certainly seems set up to make a point, but what, finally, is
Williams's lesson? What are we to think about John and Alma? The
Doctor ends up dedicated to his work and to the community, yet there
is no joy in the character; Williams does not present the Doctor's safe,
bourgeois life as an ideal. Williams celebrates Alma's release from the
rectory, just as he celebrated his own, but in the last scene Alma seems
more like a fallen than a liberated woman. Alma's encounter with the
salesman is ominous, though Williams has maintained that Alma's passion
is healthy: "What is frustrated about loving with such white-hot intensity
that it alters the whole direction of your life, and removes you from the
parlor of an Episcopal rectory to a secret room above Moon Lake Casino?"[14]

The play's tidy surface is belied, then, by the playwright's confused
responses to his characters. Williams recognized that this play which seems
so neat but which is really ambiguous does not work, and he rewrote it.
In the new version, called *Eccentricities of a Nightingale*, characterization

and action are less intense. Rather than a Dionysian rebel, John is simply a handsome, flavorless young man whom Alma worships. With the Doctor a vaguely defined, conventional romantic hero, Alma emerges clearly as the central character. In this version Alma and John spend a night together at Moon Lake Casino; and so he becomes one of Williams's angels of mercy who offers his body to a lonely, desperate woman. Their scene together is more tender than anything in the earlier play. At first, Alma thinks their being together is a mistake: "The fire has gone out and nothing will revive it. . . . It was never much of a fire, it never really got started, and now it's out. . . . Sometimes things say things for people. . . . The fire is out, it's gone out, and you feel how the room is now, it's deathly chill." But Alma has courage: "It's another year. . . . Another stretch of time to be discovered and entered and explored, and who knows what we'll find in it? Perhaps the coming true of our most improbable dreams! I'm not ashamed of tonight! I think that you and I have been honest together, even though we failed!" As Williams writes, "something changes between them" and "the fire has miraculously revived itself, a phoenix." "Where did it come from?" Alma asks. Speaking for Williams, John says, "No one has ever been able to answer that question!"

The fire imagery may be obvious, but there is nothing comparable in *Summer and Smoke* to this subdued celebration of the flesh. The scene helps to clarify Williams's attitude toward Alma—he respects her—and it suggests that the union of the soul and the body is possible.

Though it is mellower than the earlier play, Williams still writes about the spirit and the flesh in an overexcited way, embellishing his story of the minister's daughter with symbols of stone angels and Gothic spires. "A cloudy and adolescent play," complained Wolcott Gibbs.[15] "It fails to arouse even moderate interest . . . sententious, inordinately garrulous, and ultimately as monotonous as a finger exercise on a persistent piano," wrote *Newsweek.*[16] Even at this early point in his career critics were charging that the playwright's "idiom is becoming somewhat worn."[17] But the story of Alma Winemiller was perhaps a necessary preliminary to *A Streetcar Named Desire,* Williams's most mature statement on the opposition between puritan and cavalier.[18]

Blanche Du Bois and Stanley Kowalski are Williams's most flamboyant characters, and their names are virtually synonymous with two kinds of sexuality. Delicate Blanche, virile Stanley: the feminine spirit studiously refined, achingly vulnerable; the masculine spirit ascendant, stampeding.

Blanche is the most vivid of all Williams's moth characters, those defeated by circumstance; Stanley is the ultimate version of the rugged Williams stud. The battle between these two titanic fantasy figures is the occasion of Williams's fullest play, the canon's one undoubted masterpiece, and a serious contender for the best American play ever written.

A Streetcar Named Desire is the joyous culmination of Williams's early period, since the conflict the play dramatizes marks a natural line of development from *Battle of Angels* to *You Touched Me* to the two Alma plays, *Summer and Smoke* and *Eccentricities of a Nightingale.* In each play, a panting, high-strung woman is pitted against a prodigiously sensual man. In *Streetcar* the combatants are more of a match for each other than any of the other antagonists. For all his bravado, his peacock strut, and his lord of the manor authority, Stanley is threatened by Blanche's airs and titillated by her disgust with his commonness. And for all her upper crust refinement, Blanche is drawn to Stanley's emphatic virility at the same time that she is petrified of his brutish aggressiveness. Almost unconsciously, she goes to work on her brother-in-law, coyly spraying him with her perfume, teasing him with the tickle of her furs. Sniffing warily, flexing like wrestlers warming up for the bout, these two don't need much time to understand each other.

In the deadly sex war that ensues, Stanley has the edge since he is on home ground and he is confident of the appeal of his athlete's muscles. But Blanche is a cagey fighter, armed with the well-practiced defenses of Southern charm and aristocratic decorum. Williams has said recently that "Blanche was much stronger than Kowalski. When he started to assault her, he said, 'Tiger, tiger.' She was a tiger, she had much more strength than he, and she surrendered to him out of desire."[19] A stubborn opponent, a challenge to Stanley's domination of his wife Stella, Blanche is a menacing intruder who must be expelled.

Stanley and Blanche are a solid match, then. And the playwright's own ambivalence toward both characters further evens the score. Attracted and unsettled by Stanley's animal vigor, deeply sympathetic to Blanche's sensibility and yet resentful of her promiscuity, Williams writes with a fine balance. Though he is almost always divided in his feelings about his characters, Williams here makes capital dramatic use of his contrary impulses, and *Streetcar* thrives on its ambivalences.

As in *Summer and Smoke,* the two embattled characters are allegorical figures. Blanche is a complex variation on Alma's soul-spirit, Stanley a more potent version of Dr. John Buchanan's body-spirit. Romantic Blanche and naturalistic Stanley are locked in symbolic conflict: culture fights vulgarity, and is trampled. In one of Williams's most famous set speeches, as she harangues Stella with her passionate indictment of Stanley, Blanche clearly establishes the play's conflict:

He acts like an animal, has an animal's habits! . . . Thousands and thousands of years have passed him right by, and there he is—Stanley Kowalski—survivor of the Stone Age! . . . Maybe we are a long way from being made in God's image, but . . . there has been *some* progress since then! Such things as art—as poetry and music—such kinds of new light have come into the world since then! In some kinds of people some tenderer feelings have had some little beginning! That we have got to make *grow! And *cling to, and hold as our flag! In this dark march toward whatever it is we're approaching. . . . *Don't—don't hang back with the brutes!*

This is a magnificent speech, but *Streetcar* is not a straightforward thesis drama that supports Blanche's civilization over Stanley's primitive rites. No, what gives the play its terrific energy is Williams's complicated response to his representatives of art and nature. Blanche is not merely the supremely sensitive, tortured victim; and Stanley is not simply the macho villain. Blanche is not a particularly persuasive representative of the finer things of life, for she positively radiates unhealthiness; and Stanley is not the damning representative of the pagan urge. Williams, in fact, celebrates the sensual vigor and pride that Stanley so spectacularly incarnates: "Animal joy in his being is implicit in all his movements and attitudes. Since earliest manhood the center of his life has been pleasure with women, the giving and taking of it, not with weak indulgence, dependently, but with the power and pride of a richly feathered male bird among hens." Williams has said that he was so "delighted" with Stanley that he could "hardly hold him within bounds."[20]

Always evaluating his characters according to the degree of their sexual freedom, Williams gives points to Stanley for his direct, simple, healthy enjoyment of fleshly pleasure, and he subtracts points from Blanche for her sexual duplicity, her double life, for the fact that a tiger woman lurks guiltily beneath the decorous, prissy mask. Blanche loses the contest, and her defeat has a double significance, for Williams wants to indicate, as Irwin Shaw wrote, that "beauty is shipwrecked on the rock of the world's vulgarity,"[21] but he also wants to punish Blanche for her dishonest and promiscuous sex life. Blanche is two things at once: she is Williams's spokeswoman for Beauty, and she is also one of his erring protagonists who are damned for their sexual excess and maladjustment. That Blanche fails to integrate the double strand of her nature, fails to reconcile the lady with the bohemian, is at the root of her collapse. Studied gentility wars with raunchy sex; desire struggles with decorum; the Apollonian grace of Belle Reve, Blanche's ancestral mansion that symbolizes the Old South, is matched by joyless one-night stands at the Tarantula Arms: Blanche is fatally schizophrenic.

When she arrives in honky-tonk New Orleans, shadowed by the loss of Belle Reve, by her dismissal from school for having seduced a student, and by her eviction from a flea-bag hotel, she tries to disguise the truth about herself with the trappings of antebellum charm. To escape from the nagging memory of cheap sex in rundown hotels, she clings to social niceties, the tag ends of a shabby genteel heritage. Like Amanda in *The Glass Menagerie*, she idealizes the Old South world of gentlemen callers and lawn parties and liveried servants carrying silver coffee service. At the end of her rope, retreating to her sister's as the last refuge against a world that has mocked and hounded her, Blanche depends on manner, on affected little-girl innocence, to sustain her. Her ultimate defense is to turn the genteel past into art. Shading the harsh glare from the naked overhanging light, she is the perennial Williams illusion-seeker, the self-styled poet of the emotions for whom the truth kills.

For Blanche, afraid of life as it is, sex is cancerous, the chief means, along with alcohol, of her self-destruction. Sex is Blanche's way of punishing herself for her betrayal of her homosexual husband, a sensitive poet with "a softness and tenderness which wasn't like a man's, although he wasn't the least bit effeminate looking." When she discovered him with another man, Blanche rejected her husband, and like Brick in *Cat on a Hot Tin Roof,* who betrays his friend Skipper when Skipper reveals that he is homosexual, she pays dearly for her crime. In both plays betrayal of the defenseless homosexual is the supreme sin. Brick drinks himself into a daze, and Blanche gives her body away, expiating her responsibility for her husband's suicide (as Williams has said) "through her continual orgy with those boys of the army camp."[22]

For Blanche, as for many Williams characters, sex and the death wish mingle in uneasy communion. "They told me to take a streetcar named Desire, and then transfer to one called Cemeteries," she says, prophetically, as she enters the play, "and ride six blocks and get off at—Elysian Fields." But pagan Elysia, where life and sex are above, are before, good and evil, will always elude Blanche, who is obsessed with her own guilt. Her continual baths are her pathetic attempt to revive herself, but, as Williams says, "she is an hysteric, on a collision course with some terrible thing in her that Stanley brought to a head."[23] Blanche is hopelessly beyond the point where life and desire are one and good.

Williams, deeply moralistic, punishes Blanche for betraying a homosexual and for being promiscuous. He certainly identifies with her and feels compassion for her—she is one of his outsiders, an aesthete hounded by the brutes of the world—but she is a Woman With a Past, and he judges her almost as harshly as Henry Arthur Jones and Arthur Wing Pinero regarded their notorious Mrs. Ebbsmiths and Mrs. Tanquerays. Blanche is a poor soul, but she has been sinful, and so she must end unhappily.

The play, then, is written from a conservative premise. Like Williams himself, the characters are shocked and offended by Blanche's sex life, once it is uncovered. They are unforgiving, regarding her as immoral rather than sick; she is someone who must be expelled so that the moral order may continue as it was. The revelation of Blanche's sordid past seals her fate. Repressed and courtly Mitch, Stanley's one decent friend, "a he-man mama's boy,"[24] and her last chance at happiness, rejects her as insensitively as she rejected her husband. Blindly obeying the double standard and believing her every man's rightful property, Stanley seduces her ("we've had this date from the beginning"). Blanche's disclosed sinfulness moves Stella finally to choose her husband over her sister, and she begins to think of Blanche as someone outside society. Her uncovered sexual identity pushes Blanche over the edge; once her secret life has been revealed, Blanche stumbles into madness as the ultimate refuge.

A double life, hidden and ashamed sex—there is certainly evidence here to support those who read the play as a kind of pre-gay liberation homosexual nightmare with Blanche cast as an effeminate male attracted to and uncovered by Stanley, and with Stanley in the role of a threatened hard-hat bigot, a naive homosexual's fantasy of what a real man is really like, a young girl's vision of the male as muscular rapist, who must destroy the intruder in order to preserve his own masculine self-image. Acting out her charade against a society in which homosexuality is an unmentionable disease, Blanche might be interpreted as a guilt-ridden gay for whom exposure means utter humiliation. From this angle, *Streetcar* is the kind of old-fashioned play in which being gay means going crazy or committing suicide in the last act. Williams insists that Blanche is not a drag queen, and indeed the character does play as a distinctly Williams sort of woman, high-strung and fluttery. If she's not a man, though, Blanche is at least a woman's parody of a woman, a quaint and exaggeratedly feminine version of antebellum girlhood. The play has been accepted by audiences throughout the world as a potent heterosexual conflict, but to ignore the possibility that the play itself is as masked as its beleaguered heroine, is to miss reverberations that echo throughout the Williams canon.

Stripped, Blanche goes mad, and Stanley finally gets the dame who called him common. He wins; the brute stalks the earth unchecked. Williams appreciates Blanche's culture and he certainly sympathizes with her as a born victim, but he chooses Stanley: the materialist triumphs over the romantic. The outcome of the clash is presented, however, as grim necessity rather than joyous victory. Williams makes it clear that he considers realism a limited approach to life, but whether we like it or not, we must, finally, accept it.

The world left to the Kowalskis is a grisly prospect. Stanley is a better superintendent than Blanche, but he is not a hero. That he is titanic in bed excuses a lot for Stella (and for Williams too), but it cannot excuse everything. Stella lives for the colored lights at night; the joys of the low moans are enough to keep her married to Stanley. Conditioned to equate the natural with the good, we too may like Stanley—at first. His caustic wit is an antidote to Blanche's fussy pretenses. But Stanley is more the pitiless victor than the noble savage, and his willful destruction of a lost girl-woman convicts him to the ranks of Williams's cads.

Marlon Brando played the role so persuasively that we have come mistakenly to think of Kowalski as an early fifties rebel. Robert Brustein noted that Brando's Kowalski was in fact so "appealing," "sympathetic," and "sensitive" that "the villain of the piece became the prototype for a hero, the inarticulate hero of popular culture."[25] In the final round, however, though the spoils may go to Stanley, it is Blanche who claims our sympathy.

This heady, driving, wrenching play is not a plain moral fable, then. Thickly textured, with its ambivalent distribution of rewards and punishments, its complex pattern of sympathy and disapproval, its insecure, magnetic conqueror and its demented, strong-willed victim, A Streetcar Named Desire is one of the most charged and fevered works in American drama, a play that rides high on its own unresolved ambiguities and resounding internal clashes.

3

INTERLUDE

A PORTRAIT OF THE ARTIST
AS A YOUNG MAN

After his defeat with *Battle of Angels,* Williams went underground for five years. Between 1940 and 1945, he was in Hollywood as a scriptwriter, but projects for Lana Turner and Margaret O'Brien were unsuccessful, and he was never able to sign his name to any film during this period. He traveled, he collaborated with Donald Windham on *You Touched Me;* he wrote one-acts; he worked sporadically at an array of odd jobs—waiter, usher, shoe salesman; he hovered over *Battle of Angels;* and, most important of all, he wrote a screenplay, *The Gentleman Caller,* which, being roundly rejected by Metro-Goldwyn-Mayer, he turned into a play called *The Glass Menagerie.*

Unlike *Battle of Angels, The Glass Menagerie* is a warm play. A realistic family portrait laced with the poetry of mood-memory monologues, it is a domestic drama very much in the American tradition.[1] The play is a conventional autobiographical reminiscence whereas *Battle of Angels* was lopsided and quirky. *The Glass Menagerie* is a much neater play, but happily Williams chose to write all of his following plays in the manner of his early failure rather than that of his first success. Williams recalls that after the play opened in 1945, he said to a magazine reporter with "unconscious clairvoyance, 'I may not have any more nice things to say.' I must have known unconsciously that I would never write that kind of tender play again."[2] The qualities of tenderness and lyricism that dominate *The Glass Menagerie* are perennial Williams trademarks, but they are never again to be present without twisted sex and violence, for Williams's characters, from 1945 to the present, inhabit a more tortured world than the one his Wingfield family lives in.

The Glass Managerie is a memory play in which the narrator regards his unhappy mother and sister with a mixture of guilt and sentimentality. Tom is a would-be poet who feels trapped by his family and his plain job in a shoe factory. His domineering mother holds on to memories of her lost youth and a genteel past that conflicts harshly with the reduced circumstances of the present. His sister is both physically and spiritually crippled; she hides in the dim family apartment creating a fantasy world with her glass menagerie figurines. These haunted characters are variations on Williams's own unhappy family: his genteel, overbearing mother; his mostly absent father who is a towering, threatening figure nonetheless; and his schizophrenic sister Rose.

Tom reacts to his family in much the same way Williams feels about his—like the playwright himself, the narrator appreciates his mother, is estranged from his father, and is attached most of all to his fragile sister. Absorbed by the problems of his family and drawn into its female-dominated life, the fictional Tom Wingfield, like the real Tom Williams, must leave. As a poet, he must free himself of family ties; and the play celebrates his escape from the doomed family whose image pursues him as he travels, gathering experiences to be shaped into art:

Perhaps I am walking along a street at night, in some strange city, before I have found companions. I pass the lighted window of a shop where perfume is sold. The window is filled with pieces of colored glass, tiny transparent bottles in delicate colors, like bits of a shattered rainbow. Then all at once my sister touches my shoulder. I turn around and look into her eyes. . . . Oh, Laura, Laura, I tried to leave you behind me, but I am more faithful than I intended to be! I reach for a cigarette, I cross the street, I run into the movies or a bar, I buy a drink, I speak to the nearest stranger—anything that can blow your candles out!

The Glass Menagerie dramatizes Williams's younger self through the character of Tom: "Yes, I have tricks in my pocket, I have things up my sleeve. But I am the opposite of a stage magician. He gives you illusion that has the appearance of truth. I give you truth in the pleasant disguise of illusion." Tom, the genial, low-key master of ceremonies who offers us his family life in dramatic form, is analogous to the witch-like women who tend the museum in *Battle of Angels* because, like them, he guides us through the play. But Tom is a likable custodian, soft-spoken and gentle, whereas the women are mercenary scandal-mongers. Accordingly, the story they introduce is gaudy and dark while Tom's drama is presented in a whisper. The women want us to be shocked; Tom wants us to be moved. Evolving from these two early antithetical plays, Williams's subsequent work mingles titillation with tenderness; combines the grotesque with the lyrical; mixes violence with romance.

Announcer and master puppeteer, Tom keeps himself on the sidelines while reserving the spotlight for his mother and sister. He remains a shadowy figure, the sensitive poet of theatrical convention. Weaving in and out of the action and selecting the order and duration of the scenes, he is the unobtrusive stage manager who quietly observes and comments on a day of crisis in the lives of his mother and sister.

Tom's mother, Amanda, is the central character. (Laurette Taylor's performance as Amanda, the first of a series of magnificent star roles that Williams has created, is one of the legends of the American theater.[3]) Amanda is one of the playwright's most vivid Southern belles, but she differs from Blanche Du Bois or Alma Winemiller in being remarkably practical. She is very much aware of the world, and her main goal in life is to communicate that awareness to her painfully shy daughter. "Jobs" and "husbands" figure prominently in her conversation, even as she reminiscences about the refined Southern tradition in which she was raised. The character has usually been called a fluttering belle when in fact she is tough-minded and resilient. She manages her house and raises her children without a husband to help her, in circumstances far more modest than she is used to, and she never succumbs to despair. Her one real indulgence is her occasional reminiscence of her aristocratic Southern upbringing.

The memory that does most to refresh her is the one of the Sunday afternoon in Blue Mountain when she received seventeen gentlemen callers. The image that most revives her is that of the Mississippi Delta in May, "all lacy with dogwood, literally flooded with jonquils." Like many Williams characters, she is past her prime, yet she confronts her fate with more grace and good sense than almost any of the others. In her biography of her son, Mrs. Williams has said, with ill-concealed irritation, that she is decidedly *not* Amanda Wingfield: "I'm sure if Tom stops to think, he realizes I am not. The only resemblance I have to Amanda is that we both like jonquils."[4] Yet as she describes the active social life of her youth, Mrs. Williams echoes the rhythms and the themes of Amanda's gilded speeches:

After you danced until two or three in the morning, you were not too ambitious the next day. Gathering yourself together in the afternoon, you might sit on the veranda and wait for callers. Sunday was a great day for the young men to go from house to house calling on the girls. . . . We didn't fly from one lurid romance to another as young women do today. Our relationships were rather on the basis of friendship. I wouldn't have dreamed of 'going steady,' would have found it boring.[5]

Mrs. Williams ought to be proud that her son honored her with this portrait of a woman who combines, in her own quiet way, the aesthetic sensibility of a Blanche Du Bois and the survival instinct of a Stanley Kowalski.

Amanda's daughter Laura, on the other hand, is one of Williams's pathetic victims. Too sensitive even to attend business school, she spends her time in museums and movies when the weather is harsh and strolls through parks and window-shops when it is not. Her glass menagerie symbolizes her own extreme vulnerability; yet unlike the playwright's later variations on this character type, Laura is not hopelessly lost.

Williams's memory play concentrates on a specific incident, the visit of a gentleman caller who is the symbol, as Tom describes him, of "the long delayed but always expected something that we live for." Jim, the narrator goes on to say, is "the most realistic character in the play, being an emissary from a world of reality that we were somehow set apart from." He is "a nice, ordinary, young man" whose averageness emphasizes the Wingfield family's eccentricity. But Jim, who was a high school athlete and the most popular man on campus, has already betrayed his early promise, for six years after his high school triumphs, he has only a plain job at the warehouse where Tom works. Jim has kept his genial personality, though, and he brings Laura out of herself; during the time he spends with her, he makes her seem like a normal girl. As they dance, they break the horn of the unicorn, and now Laura's favorite figurine in her glass menagerie is no different from the other horses.

Jim is the most relaxed and well-adjusted of all of Williams's male saviors. Amanda and Laura regard the handsome guest as the source of their redemption, but typically, the splendid male is beyond the reach of Williams's desperate female characters. Although Amanda and Laura lose Jim because he is already engaged, his presence has soothed them for a time. Like *A Streetcar Named Desire*, *The Glass Menagerie* dramatizes a defeat that we would give much to prevent; but Laura, like Blanche, is so used to being a victim that she cannot possibly triumph.

A warm play, deeply personal and yet shrewdly shaped for popular appeal, *The Glass Menagerie* is a detour for Williams, a calm moment between the flamboyant melodrama of *Battle of Angels* and the high-strung combats of *Summer and Smoke* and *A Streetcar Named Desire.* *The Glass Menagerie* is a typical autobiographical play, yet it is clearly the work of a unique sensibility. All of the usual elements of a Williams play are here, but in no other drama has Williams written in the mellowed, autumnal tone of this American perennial.

4

DEPARTURES

By 1950 Williams's reputation as the playwright of Southern frustration was almost too firmly established. Whether in response to the critical complaints that he was repeating himself or to his own artistic needs, Williams experimented with new styles and themes in the period from 1950 to 1956. Loneliness and sexual maladjustments are still the main concerns of these plays, but the spirit—and in the case of *Camino Real,* the form—are different from his earlier work.

The Rose Tattoo (1951) at least tries for a happier depiction of sex than any of the preceding plays. A rowdy, lusty comedy, it was inspired by Williams's pleasurable visit, in the late forties, to Italy, a country he has always idealized as the embodiment of healthy sensuality. "I have felt more hopeful about human nature as a result of being exposed to the Italians," Williams said at the time. *The Rose Tattoo,* he maintained, was directly influenced "by the vitality, humanity, and love of life expressed by the Italian people."[1]

After he had written *The Rose Tattoo,* Williams began *Camino Real* (1953), his most experimental work, a sprawling, free-form fantasia on themes and character types that appear throughout his plays. In this extravaganza, Williams is still detained by conflicts that preoccupied him in the forties, but this time he frames his drama in a novel format. *Camino Real* is the playwright's one orchestral composition, and it remains one of his favorite plays. He has called it his "major" statement about "the life and times we live in."

The critics were puzzled, and in his next play, Williams returned to more conventional territory. *Cat on a Hot Tin Roof* (1955) is a salty domestic melodrama that is more optimistic than the dark plays of the *Streetcar–Summer and Smoke* period. *Baby Doll,* Williams's screenplay for the 1956 movie (a fusion of two one-act plays) is delightfully perverse, an ornery, downbeat depiction of sex and greed among some dim-witted Southerners. *Baby Doll* and *Cat on a Hot Tin Roof* are two of Williams's most enjoyable works; *The Rose Tattoo* is a misfire and *Camino Real* a nuisance, but on the whole this was a productive period for the playwright.

Williams announced before its opening that *The Rose Tattoo* would be noticeably free of neurotic spinsters and sexual torment. "If anyone mentions 'neurotic' in connection with this play, I'll reach for a gun," he said.[2] While it is true that the play contains no half-crazed Southern belles, its Sicilian heroine is still far from being a picture of tranquil mental health. High-strung and thick-headed, Serafina della Rose is one of the playwright's most obsessed characters—like several of Williams's sex-worshippers, she is a passionate puritan. Idealizing her late husband and enshrining his ashes, she lives like a nun in a cloister, isolated from her Sicilian Gulf Coast community and exacting from her daughter an unreasonable abstinence. She is a dressmaker who sews and stitches for festive occasions in which she takes no part.

Serafina, in short, is no less disturbed than any of Williams's earlier heroines; but since he has called the play a comedy, he is obliged to provide his character with a happy ending. Serafina is cured of her obsession with the memory of her husband when she learns from gossips that he was unfaithful. She falls in love with a lusty man who, like her husband, drives a banana truck. In the last act, she is saved by sex.

With its sensual banana truck drivers, its hot-blooded heroine, its volatile Sicilian community, and its panting juveniles in the grip of the sex urge (Serafina's daughter Rose and her sailor boyfriend), *The Rose Tattoo* is a near-parody of Williams's overheated style. Harold Clurman suggested that Williams was trying "to solve a certain aspect of his inner problem by writing about a group of characters who are less burdened with the subjective ambivalence and the tormented Puritanism of his more purely American characters. Williams has tried here to free himself of some of the tensions he suffers at home by writing objectively, so to speak, of strangers."[3] Williams himself said that in this play he was "attempting something outside [his] own personal feelings."[4]

Serafina is "a hymn of praise to the unfettered sexual instinct."[5]

More than any other character in the canon, she worships the healing power of sex, worships it with such passion and single-mindedness that for her sex is a kind of transcendence: "To me the big bed was beautiful like a religion." Her shrine is the urn containing her husband's ashes. Her husband died three years ago, but memories of her nights with him sustain her:

I remember my husband with a body like a young boy and hair on his head as thick and black as mine is and skin on him smooth and sweet as a yellow rose petal. At night I sit here and I'm satisfied to remember, because I had the best. . . . And I would feel cheap and degraded and not fit to live with my daughter or under the roof with the urn of his blessed ashes, those—ashes of a rose—if after that memory, after knowing that man, I went to some other, some middle-aged man, not young, not full of young passion, but getting a pot belly on him and losing his hair and smelling of sweat and liquor—and trying to fool myself that *that* was love-making! I *know* what love-making was. And I'm satisfied just to remember.

Nowhere else in the plays is the virile male so openly, so exuberantly celebrated, and nowhere else is there the same open horror of age.

Serafina is a victim of what D. H. Lawrence has called sex in the head since she wants more from the experience of sex than any earthly encounter could possibly provide. For this fierce sensualist, the pleasures of sex are closely hoarded spiritual experiences; the nights—4380 of them —with her powerful husband are her religion. A tempestuous yet oddly chaste sex-singer, she celebrates the body with a kind of virginal astonishment.

Wildly unstable, nearly driven mad by the memory of her husband, Serafina is not a likely heroine for the congenial sex comedy Williams thought he was writing. Haggling with neighborhood gossips, closeting herself behind shutters and darkened doors, preventing her daughter from having a normal girlhood romance, Serafina dominates the first part of the play like a Medea of the Gulf Coast. She is a big dramatic character (forcefully played by Maureen Stapleton on stage and Anna Magnani on film), and Williams hasn't found a fable large enough to accommodate her. After we have been introduced to Serafina's antisocial behavior, the play plunges from high drama to farce. Williams brings on a rugged truck driver, named Angelo Mangiacavallo (Eat-a-horse) who is the medicine for Serafina's melancholy: "Love and affection is what I got to offer on hot or cold days in this lonely old world," he advertises, "and is what I am looking for. I got nothing else." Once this fantasy stud enters the play, it becomes bawdy and relaxed; but the broad sexual comedy isn't consistent with the highly charged first act in which Serafina has been established as a seriously maladjusted character.

The becalmed Serafina at the end of the play is too far removed from the character as we first see her. Walter Kerr noted that "the heroine . . . has been presented to us as a quicksilver compound of physical passion, intense idealism, and hysterical religiosity. That a single sexual act should reduce these qualities to a happy harmony is implausible."[6] The formula Broadway finale is not convincing because the playwright, like his volcanic heroine, is not comfortable with the norm. Serafina constantly rebels against Williams's story line just as the play resists Williams's attempt to turn it into a comedy.

The Rose Tattoo is never safe from the threat of self-parody. The underlying silliness is particularly evident in Williams's obsessive use of roses. As John Mason Brown noted, "not since the Houses of York and Lancaster feuded long and publicly have roses been used more lavishly than by Mr. Williams. . . . Roses are mystical signs, proofs of passion, symbols of devotion . . . so many cheap flowers [are] used to fancy up a lot of downright foolishness."[7] Roses connote for Williams a full, guiltless sensuality. The rose tattoo that decorates the chest of Serafina's husband is the mark of his superior virility. The night she conceived, Serafina imagines she saw an identical rose tattoo on her own chest—an obvious emblem of her intense identification with her husband. She is tricked into believing in Angelo's compatibility when he sports a rose tattoo on *his* chest: "The rose is the heart of the world like the heart is the—heart of the—body!" he croons. Estelle Hohengarten, the mistress of Serafina's husband, is identified by the rose tattoo on her chest. Serafina's last name is della Rose; her husband is Rosario della Rose; her daughter is Rosa della Rose. The epidemic of roses pinpoints the play's uneasy straddling of low comedy and high mysticism.

Camino Real is Williams's most elaborate play. It is his great bid for High Art in which he tries to be poetic and philosophical. Though there are beautiful passages, the play contains some of his most shrill and precious writing and happily, Williams does not write again in such an inflated style until *Out Cry,* which was conceived during his breakdown period in the late sixties.

In *Camino Real* Williams has constructed a full-scale fantasy version of the world view popularized by his forties plays. In his foreword Williams defines the play's imaginary setting as "the construction of . . . a separate existence . . . it is nothing more nor less than my conception of the time and world that I live in." As in *A Streetcar Named Desire,* it is a world in which the aesthetes and the dreamers are pursued by the brutes. A collection of the playwright's lonely and dispossessed characters, his has-beens and his eternal victims, are trapped at the end of the road where the Royal Highway becomes the Real Way, in a grimy, forlorn town "in an unspecified Latin-American country" surrounded menacingly by the Terra Incognita, a vast and presumably impassable desert. As in the forties plays, it is a world sharply divided between the vulnerable dreamers and the tough realists; between the rich, sheltered clientele at the Siete Mares Hotel and the Skid Row bums, the hucksters and the loan sharks at the facing flea-bag Ritz Men Only.

Isolated in this exotic no man's land are the playwright's usual assortment of misfits, disguised as literary and historical figures like Byron, Marguerite Gautier, Casanova, and Kilroy. The play's most familiar of Williams's types are Gautier, a once-legendary courtesan who now has to pay for affection, and Casanova, a once-splendid lover now penniless and wearing the cuckold's horns. They are both aging voluptuaries who recall their former glory while trying to cope with their reduced circumstances. Gautier, the Lady of the Camellias, a Blanche Du Bois raised to the level of myth, embodies "the legend of the sentimental whore." She has escaped from Bide-a-While, "one of those places with open sleeping verandahs . . . [with] rows and rows of narrow white iron beds as regular as tombstones." Shunned by the aristocratic clientele of the Siete Mares, Casanova instructs Marguerite "to carry the banner of Bohemia into the enemy camp."

Kilroy is the Williams wanderer. Based on the legendary World War II character, Williams's Kilroy is the quintessential American innocent; he's good-natured and trusting, and he is thoroughly abused as he passes through the Camino Real. Like Casanova and Marguerite, Kilroy is an also-ran, a former champ who had to give up the prizefight game because of his heart that's as big as the head of a baby. Kilroy is the eternal dupe, the perennial clown, the token patsy. Williams's least neurotic hero, he's been "had for a button! Stewed, screwed and tattooed on the Camino Real! Baptized, finally, with the contents of a slopjar!—Did anybody say the deal was rugged?" Dressed in a clown suit and selected as the hero of the hour (he gets to spend forty-five minutes with Esmeralda, the Gypsy's daughter), he's robbed, beaten, and humiliated, only to be cornered at last by the Streetcleaners, the town's omnipresent emissaries of death. Cocky to the end, Kilroy meets the ghouls with a challenge: "Come on, you sons of bitches! Kilroy is here! He's ready!"

Like Kilroy, Williams's Lord Byron also fights the destructive and violent world of the Camino Real. Byron is a sophisticated version of the boyish, hillbilly Kilroy. Alone among the entrapped characters, Byron, the eternal yea-sayer, has the courage to confront the terra incognita. Byron is the first of a Williams archetype—the artist in decline, the poet whose gifts are corrupted by worldliness:

That was my vocation once [to influence the heart . . . to purify it and lift it above its ordinary level] . . . before it was obscured by vulgar plaudits!—Little by little it was lost among gondolas and palazzos!— masked balls, glittering salons, huge shadowy courts and torch-lit entrances!—Baroque facades, canopies and carpets, candelabra and gold plate among snowy damask, ladies with throats as slender as flower-stems, bending and breathing toward me their fragrant breath—Exposing their breasts to me!

Byron wants to escape the "passion for declivity in this world" and to hear again "the single—pure—stringed instrument of my heart." "Make voyages!" is his theme, and limping across the plaza "with his head bowed, making slight, apologetic gestures to the wheedling Beggars who shuffle about him . . . he crosses to the steep Alleyway Out."

Byron, Kilroy, Gautier, and Casanova, victims of a brutish universe, are among Williams's most positive strugglers, and the playwright rewards them all. Byron escapes, heroically, the tarnished artist in search of his mislaid gifts. After periods of distrust and betrayal, Gautier and Casanova turn to each other for comfort. And Kilroy, resurrected, braves the terra incognita as the Sancho Panza to Don Quixote, the cavalier knight whose dream this play is:

I'll sleep and dream for a while against the wall of this town. . . . And my dream will be a pageant, a masque in which old meanings will be remembered and possibly new ones discovered, and when I wake from this sleep and this disturbing pageant of a dream, I'll choose one among its shadows to take along with me in the place of Sancho.

The old lovers, the declining artist, and the former boxer are Quixote's dreamers stranded in a decrepit town presided over by the evil proprietor of the Siete Mares, Señor Gutman. The devil to Quixote's saint, Gutman is one of Williams's threatening paternal figures, the embodiment of the town's venality and cynicism. With faceless, death-wielding Streetcleaners lurking around every darkened corner, with its neon-lit garishness and its casual violence, the town is a high fantasy version of Williams's original setting, the destructive community of bigots in *Battle of Angels.* Good battles evil in Nightmare City, and wins, since Williams's victims triumph over the forces of darkness. The play's final image, "the violets in the mountains have broken the rocks," suggests the victory of the romantics, the children of Quixote, over the cynics. *Camino Real* is to some extent the optimistic play that Williams promised in *The Rose Tattoo;* but until the final uplift, when the downtrodden characters are released from their imprisonment, the play is grim. Williams has said that *Camino Real* is "a picture of the state of the romantic non-conformist in modern society. It stresses honor and man's own sense of inner dignity which the Bohemian must reachieve after each period of degradation he is bound to run into."[8] Resurrection is the play's main theme: Kilroy rises, phoenix-like, from his own cadaver, reborn as companion in adventure to Don Quixote. And as a low comedy parallel, the Gypsy's daughter is turned magically into a virgin with the rising of each full moon.

Williams's "plea for a romantic attitude toward life"[9] depends on schematic separations. Good confronts evil in a more direct way than in plays like *A Streetcar Named Desire* or even *Summer and Smoke. Camino Real* is structured like a medieval morality drama with Kilroy an Everyman whose soul is saved not because of his unshakable belief in God but because he has integrity. Kilroy is threatened, tempted, harassed by sharp-shooters and con men, but he is never corrupted. Beneath its elaborate window dressing, *Camino Real* is one of Williams's most simplistic statements. As Harold Clurman noted: "Far from being obscure, the play reiterates its intention and meaning at every point. In fact, it is too nakedly clear to be a sound work of art."[10]

Filled with spectacle and action, the play is a kind of theatrical circus, a festival of song and dance, of vaudevillian routines and music hall patter. In his foreword, Williams notes that "in these following pages [is] only the formula by which a play could exist." Dependent on "form and color and line . . . light and motion," *Camino Real* is in fact complete only in performance. Eric Bentley cited the production as proof of the wicked fascination of [its director] Elia Kazan.... Kazan goes to work on the actors' nerves like an egg beater.... Yet it's no use knowing he is not a good director unless you can also see that he is almost a great one.... He is a showman ... there is no doubt that Kazan has found his own way of lifting a performance above the trivial and naturalistic. Conversely, when the action tends towards the artifice of dance or ceremony, he knows how to keep it anchored in everyday reality.[11]

The play's language matches its procession of theatrical effects. Opening all the stops on his verbal keyboard, Williams is lyrical, colloquial, airy, raffish, vulgar. Byron's long monologue, exhorting the characters to "make voyages," is written in a lush prose, while the Gypsy speaks in a tough, Madison Avenue jargon:

There's nobody left to uphold the old traditions! You raise a girl. She watches television. Plays be-bop. Reads *Screen Secrets*. Comes the Big Fiesta. The moonrise makes her a virgin—which is the neatest trick of the week! And what does she do? Chooses a Fugitive Patsy for the Chosen Hero! Well, show him in! Admit the joker and get the virgin ready! ... I'm operating a legitimate joint! This joker'll get the same treatment he'd get if he breezed down the Camino in a blizzard of G-notes! Trot, girl! Lubricate your means of locomotion!

Throughout the play, Williams uses a blend of poetic and pop diction that is intended to startle the audience. Sometimes, the language has an agreeable staccato rhythm; at other times, it is flat or bloated.

There are some lovely set speeches (Byron's credo, Esmeralda's blessing on the play's victims)[12] and some theatrically exciting scenes (Esmeralda's comic seduction of Kilroy; the Fiesta; Gautier's desperate attempt to get on the unscheduled plane that offers escape from her prison). As a whole, however, the play is forced and affected. From time to time, Williams has claimed that this is his favorite play, but he was more accurate when he called it "a mutilated play. It had my best writing in it. But there were things in it that didn't quite seem rational, even in terms of the wildness of the play."[13]

Cat on a Hot Tin Roof (1955) marks Williams's return to commercial melodrama. The subject—a woman desires a handsome, unattainable male —is familiar, but in this play the male is more disturbed than the woman. Maggie the Cat in fact is one of Williams's healthiest characters. When he first started working on the character, for a short story called "Four Players of a Summer Game," he depicted her as a mannish, dominating wife. But as he began writing the play, he softened her; and when Elia Kazan asked him to make her even more sympathetic, Williams readily complied: "Kazan felt that the character of Margaret, while he understood that I sympathized with her and liked her myself, should be, if possible, more clearly sympathetic to an audience. . . . I embraced [this suggestion] whole-heartedly from the outset, because it so happened that Maggie the Cat had become steadily more charming to me as I worked on her characterization."[14] Like most of Williams's women, Maggie wants her man, and she goes after him vigorously. As twitchy as a cat on a hot tin roof, Maggie is the passionate Williams woman, aching for possession of the spectacular Williams man; but she is not a grotesque. She is neither a faded mother figure nor a puritan in tortured rebellion against her heritage, but a normal, likable woman who loves her distracted husband.

Brick, like his prototype Val Xavier, is the withdrawn stud who wants to be free of claims on his body. Brick does not want to go to bed with his wife, and this is the play's central conflict and its central mystery. What is Brick's problem? It is clear, first of all, that Brick is a case of arrested development since he still wants to think he's a football hero. Hobbling through the play on a crutch (he has injured himself trying to relive a heroic moment on the football field), Brick is both literally and symbolically crippled.

His real problem, though, is Skipper. He and Skipper were fellow athletes who had a "deep understanding." In order to pry Brick away from his friend, Maggie accused Skipper of being homosexual, and bullied him into going to bed with her to prove that he wasn't. He failed, and when he called Brick to tell him, Brick hung up on Skipper in disgust. Skipper killed himself, and Brick can't forget his betrayal of his friend. Withdrawing from his wife and family, he refuses to sleep with Maggie or to challenge his brother Gooper for the estate of their rich, dying father.

In its shifty and evasive treatment of Brick's possible homosexuality, *Cat on a Hot Tin Roof* is clearly a pre-gay liberation play in which the possibility that a character might be "that way" is enough to give him a nervous breakdown. The play offers a grim choice to the actual or potential homosexual: he can either kill himself or drink himself into a stupor. The burden of his possible homosexuality is too much for Brick to confront, and, on the evidence of his treatment of it in the play, it was too much at the time for Williams as well. The playwright, in a statement he would now scoff at, denied that the play is about homosexuality at all:

> Brick is definitely not homosexual. . . . Brick's self-pity and recourse to the bottle are not the result of a guilty conscience. . . . He feels that the collapse and premature death of his great friend Skipper . . . have been caused by unjust attacks on his moral character made by outsiders, including . . . the wife. It is his bitterness at Skipper's tragedy that has caused Brick to turn against his wife and find solace in drink, rather than any personal involvement, although I do suggest that, at least at some time in his life, there have been unrealized abnormal tendencies.[15]

On a later occasion Williams even more defensively explained "the truth" of the play: "Critics often wander off when it comes to my plays. I have heard *Cat on a Hot Tin Roof* described as being about homosexuality, but it isn't—it's about people having to live out lies."[16]

Whatever labels are attached to it, Brick's sexual maladjustment is at the center of the play. All of the characters are constantly fussing over it, clucking their tongues in astonishment and disapproval; and the audience is placed in the position of wondering is he or isn't he? The Pollitt household is a hotbed of raging heterosexuals for whom the possibility of an "unnatural" attachment between Brick and his friend is as much a menace as the cancer that is killing Big Daddy. At times Williams seems to approach homosexuality with the same mixture of astonishment and revulsion expressed by his deeply conservative, society-bound characters; at other times, he seems to celebrate the friendship that Brick has idealized: "Skipper and me had a clean, true thing between us!—had a clean friendship, practically all our lives, till Maggie got the idea you're talking about. Normal? No!—It was too rare to be normal, any true thing between two people is too rare to be normal."

Brick, at any rate, is not comfortable with his sexuality, and Williams presents his maladjustment as the result of indoctrination by a smug and intolerant straight society. When Brick asks his father, "Why can't exceptional friendship, *real, real, deep, deep friendship!* between two men be respected as something clean and decent without being thought of as— *Fairies,*" Williams adds a significant comment: "In his utterance of this word, we gauge the wide and profound reach of the conventional mores he got from the world that crowned him with early laurel." Is *Cat on a Hot Tin Roof,* as Marion Magid asked, a play "about a man unjustly accused by a society which is right (yes, homosexuality is evil, but this wasn't it) or a play about a man justly accused by a society which is wrong (no, homosexuality is not evil, it is only wicked tongues that make it out to be so)?"[17] Is Brick condemned for betraying Skipper? Is Brick self-deluded? Or is he instead pure in heart, a hold-out against the vulgar bourgeois family that hounds him?

In the act 2 confrontation between father and son, Williams edges warily toward a direct treatment of the fearful subject. Big Daddy is a redneck patriarch, yet he is sympathetic to Brick's sexual indecisiveness, and he seems to want to coax Brick into making a confession. Trying to reach each other for the first time in their lives, father and son approach the forbidden topic gingerly. Big Daddy agrees with Brick about the beauty of a pure, clean, male friendship, but he presses further, wanting to focus a full and steady light on the troublesome theme at last. At the moment of direct attack, however, Brick tosses in a diversionary tactic by brutally telling Big Daddy the truth about his cancer. This shift from one taboo subject (homosexuality) to another (cancer), which effectively ends Big Daddy's probe into the story of Brick and Skipper, is the most dishonest moment in all of Williams's plays. As if in defense of his evasion of the subject, Williams explains in a parenthetical note:

The bird that I hope to catch in the net of this play is not the solution of one man's psychological problem. I'm trying to catch the true quality of experience in a group of people, that cloudy, flickering, evanescent— fiercely charged!—interplay of live human beings in the thundercloud of a common crisis. Some mystery should be left in the revelation of character in a play, just as a great deal of mystery is always left in the revelation of character in life, even in one's own character to himself.

As in the play itself, Williams is obscuring the real subject of his drama with fevered language, and this plea for "mystery" is a shabby ploy.

Williams is as afraid of the truth as Brick is. The play confronts the truth that Big Daddy is dying of cancer; Brick speaks the truth to Big Daddy; Gooper announces the truth to Big Mama. But is Brick gay? That question is never answered. Eric Bentley commented that *Cat on a Hot Tin Roof* was "heralded by some as the play in which homosexuality was at last to be presented without evasion. But the miracle has still not happened."[18]

To still our doubts, and to provide a happy ending, Williams assigns Brick to Maggie's bed. In the original version, Brick agrees reluctantly to Maggie's demands. In the Kazan-inspired act 3 rewrite, Brick is much more accommodating. We are left, then, with the impression that Brick has been "cured," and yet there is nothing in the play to warrant his magical transformation. And Williams knows it since in his note to the revised act 3 he states his own disbelief in Brick's conversion:

I felt that the moral paralysis of Brick was a root thing in his tragedy . . . to show a dramatic progression would obscure the meaning of that tragedy. . . . I don't believe that a conversation, however revelatory, ever effects so immediate a change in the heart or conduct of a person in Brick's state of spiritual disrepair. However, I wanted Kazan to direct the play. . . . I was fearful that I would lose his interest if I didn't re-examine the script from his point of view.

Williams's agreement with Kazan's demands indicates his own discomfort with the material. Bringing Brick into the family community is a much less painful ending than leaving him isolated outside it; for both the playwright and his audience, the image of Brick as an acquiescent family man is more digestible than that of Brick as a tortured rebel.

That Brick might be homosexual made everyone connected with the play nervous. When Richard Brooks made the film version, the homosexual theme was even more rigorously denied; Brooks claimed that "there was no indication by Williams that Brick was a homosexual." Brooks identified the character's problem as "his reluctance to grow up." The film's veiled treatment of Brick and Skipper's friendship makes us wonder what is troubling the hero, after all.

But in both the film and the play, no matter how strenuously it is avoided, the subject of homosexuality intrudes on the bustling comedy-melodrama surface. That Brick will not sleep with his wife, that her sexual presence triggers his deep disgust, that he resents her for breaking up his friendship with Skipper, that he is touchy whenever Skipper's name is mentioned—all these facts cannot be disregarded. Further, in his script Williams makes it clear that the bedroom in which the play is set was once the room of the homosexual lovers who ran the plantation—the spirits of Jack Straw and Peter Ochello hover over the play like patron saints.

Williams leaves open the possibility that sex between Maggie and Brick might be good, but he presents his *real* heterosexual couples with contempt: Gooper and Mae, forever boasting of their fertility, are thoroughly unappealing, and their shrieking, squawking brood of no-neck monsters is hardly calculated to advance the cause of child rearing. The marriage of Big Daddy and Big Mama is equally unsatisfactory since Big Daddy despises and ridicules his fat wife, while Big Mama takes the insults and the jeers and yet blindly worships her husband.

Try as he may to disguise it, Williams's true sympathy is reserved for that idealized friendship between Brick and Skipper, a communion that none of the play's heterosexual relationships can match. Williams appreciates Maggie, but even she cannot come up to the level of communication shared by the friends. She is the intruder in the clean, pure, male entente, the cat (the whore) who destroys the friendship with her female lust. Unable, in 1955, to write openly the paean to homosexual love that the material contains, Williams has instead directed a satiric glance at an obnoxious, male-chauvinist household, and the result is a sardonic, masked comedy-drama instead of a serious exploration of a guilt-ridden homosexual.

Williams had a chance in this play to write a thoughtful drama on the fears and insecurities of a homosexual in a conservative society, but as is, *Cat on a Hot Tin Roof* is no more helpful than the execrable *Tea and Sympathy:* both plays try to comfort Broadway audiences with the assurance that homosexuality is neither good nor bad, it simply doesn't exist.

It is ironic that Williams is obsessed here with the theme of mendacity. He rates his characters according to their ability to speak the truth. Big Daddy, especially, hates lies and liars, and unlike Brick, he can accept the truth about himself; he demands the truth about his illness just as Brick avoids the truth about his sexual feelings.

Although *Cat on a Hot Tin Roof* is Williams's most dishonest play, its craftsmanship is admirable. The characters are all lively, the dialogue crackles, and the action moves from one explosive encounter to another. Maggie dominates act 1 as she wittily sets the scene by sketching the family history and introduces the subject of Skipper while trying to entice Brick back to her bed. This tour de force is matched by the act 2 father-son confrontation which is a powerful scene of confession and reminiscence despite its evasiveness. Only in act 3, when it focuses on the contest between Maggie and Gooper for the estate, does the play somewhat lose its momentum; but even here it is enlivened by the tart exchanges, the wisecracks, the speed of the action.

Williams's achievement in *Cat on a Hot Tin Roof* has been to disguise a prohomosexual, antibourgeois, antiheterosexual play into a seemingly orthodox popular comedy. On the level of Broadway domestic drama, it is a skillful performance; as a treatment of the omnipresent though indirect Williams theme of the homosexual as outsider, it is a cheat.

5

THREE DARK PLAYS

Williams's three plays of the late fifties, *Orpheus Descending* (1957), *Suddenly Last Summer,* and *Sweet Bird of Youth* (1959), are sensational melodramas filled with lurid sex and violence. Williams's magnetic heroes are either lynched, eaten alive, or castrated; and his heroines are either shot or driven to the edge of insanity. Rewards and punishments are more moralistic, and more confused, in these plays of doom than anywhere else in Williams's work.

In all three plays Williams dramatizes a ruthless society. In *Orpheus Descending* and *Sweet Bird of Youth,* his characters are victimized by Southern bigots. In *Suddenly Last Summer* the characters are controlled by a decadent poet. Typically, Williams has transformed his private nightmares into commercial melodramas, and yet has expressed surprise at "the degree to which both critics and audiences have accepted his barrage of violence." After *Suddenly Last Summer* was favorably received, Williams said, "I thought I would be critically tarred and feathered and ridden on a fence rail out of the New York theatre."[1]

The play is Williams's ultimate homophile fantasy. Written during a period of intense depression (following the failure of *Orpheus Descending*), the play indicates the author's deeply ambivalent attitudes toward homosexuality (at the time). We never see the spectacularly decadent Sebastian; but his personal style sets the tone for the play and influences the action. Sebastian cuts an elegant figure. He and his mother, who is his traveling companion, are respected for their beauty and their seeming youthfulness. Like many Williams characters, the two sophisticates are obsessed with youth; as Mrs. Venable explains, "Both of us were young, and stayed young. . . . It takes character to refuse to grow old . . . —successfully to refuse it. It calls for discipline, abstention, one cocktail before dinner, not two, four, six—a single lean chop and lime juice on a salad in restaurants famed for rich dishes."

Mrs. Venable describes their attitude toward life as something

that's hardly been known in the world since the great Renaissance princes were crowded out of their palaces and gardens by successful shopkeepers! . . . Most people's lives—what are they but trails of debris, each day more debris, more debris, long, long trails of debris with nothing to clean it all up but, finally death. . . . My son, Sebastian, and I constructed our days, each day, we would—carve out each day of our lives like a piece of sculpture.—Yes, we left behind us a trail of days like a gallery of sculpture!

Traveling from the Lido to the Ritz in Madrid, to Biarritz and the Riviera, Sebastian and Violet are a famous couple. Although Williams is attracted to their luxurious life, he feels he must punish them for their easy living: he is both seduced and appalled by their decadence.

On their travels Sebastian used his mother to procure boys for him, though Mrs. Venable never seems to have been aware of her function. When she outlived her usefulness by becoming too old, Sebastian acquired his nubile cousin Catherine as the bait. Violet Venable, who could be charming and gregarious, was able to attract strangers in a way that her withdrawn son could not. But Catherine, a shapely young woman who rises out of the sea in a transparent white bathing suit, attracts a different kind of crowd than the genteel Mrs. Venable appealed to. Catherine lures a rough crowd, a group of ragged, half-naked native boys, who devour Sebastian: this is the horror that happened "suddenly last summer," and this is what is revealed to us, gradually, as first Violet and then Catherine try to reconstruct the past for the doctor whom Mrs. Venable has hired to perform a lobotomy on her distraught niece, in order to stop "her insane babblings."

The play is embellished with images of devouring. A carnivorous Venus fly trap is the prize possession of Sebastian's tropical garden in which the play is set, and Mrs. Venable tells the Doctor about sea turtles who devour their young, a nightmare scene that her son witnessed on one of their travels. "Truly," Williams said at the time the play opened, "egos eat egos, personalities eat personalities. . . . The human individual is a cannibal in the worst way.... In *Suddenly Last Summer* it was more symbolic than actual."[2] This is exactly the problem, because contrary to all elementary literary rules, the play's symbols are not anchored in reality. At the end of her confessional monologue, when she is on the verge of speaking the truth, Catherine explains: "And this you won't believe, nobody *has* believed it, nobody *could* believe it, nobody, nobody on earth could possibly believe it, and I don't *blame* them!" Williams is, in effect, apologizing for the purely fantastic nature of his story. Sebastian's being cannibalized makes sense only on a symbolic level because, as Ibsen's Judge Brack says, "people don't do such things."

Believing in a malevolent God, and living his life in homage to him, Sebastian is the consumer who is finally consumed, the cannibal who is eaten alive. His life ends as it was lived. But since the cannibalism is an actual as well as symbolic event, why, we have a right to ask, did the native boys devour him? He has taunted them, flung money at them, treated them superciliously, but, as so often in Williams, the punishment certainly seems to exceed the crime. Williams complained that the film version "made unfortunate concessions to the realism that Hollywood is too often afraid to discard. And so a short morality play, in a lyrical style, was turned into a sensationally successful film that the public thinks was a literal study of such things as cannibalism, madness, and sexual deviation."[3] But the play also confuses the literal and the symbolic, and surely, on whatever level it is read, it is about "cannibalism, madness, and sexual deviation," and not, as Williams claims, "all human confusion and its consequence: violence."

Underneath the elaborate symbolism, the play can be interpreted as a fantasy of homosexual guilt. As Arthur Ganz has written, "Sebastian is punished for what he is rather than what he does."[4] His fate expresses the ultimate fear of the cruising gay attracted to rough trade. Sebastian's cannibalization on a South American mountaintop is an exotic counterpart to the homosexual who is robbed and beaten up in a waterfront alleyway. The cannibalistic native boys resemble the Southern rednecks in *Battle of Angels* who react violently to sexual transgression. Like the heroes of several other plays, Sebastian dies in a horrible way because he has offended the sexual norm.

Williams conceals as well as expands his real subject, homosexual guilt, with belabored symbolism; Sebastian's crime and punishment are enacted in a cosmic setting. Sebastian is thus not simply a promiscuous closet homosexual, but a self-created legend who offers himself to a malevolent deity. Mrs. Venable tells the doctor that her son was always looking for God and finally saw Him in the attack on the sea turtles, a mass annihilation he witnessed in the Encantadas:

The just-hatched sea turtles scrambled out of the sand pits and started their race to the sea . . . to escape the flesh-eating birds that made the sky almost as black as the beach. And the sand all alive, all alive, as the hatched sea-turtles made their dash for the sea, while the birds hovered and swooped to attack. . . . They were diving down on the hatched sea turtles, turning them over to expose their soft undersides, tearing the undersides open and rending and eating their flesh. . . . Well, now I've said it, my son was looking for God. I mean for a clear image of Him. He spent that whole blazing equatorial day in the crow's nest of the schooner watching that thing on the beach of the Encantadas till it was too dark to see it, and when he came back down the rigging, he said, "Well, now I've seen Him!"—and he meant God. . . .

Sebastian interprets the nightmare on the beach as "the truth about the world we live in," and perversely, he lives his life—acquiring, sampling, and rejecting people like items on a menu—in confirmation of this dark "truth." Williams, therefore, tries to link Sebastian's sexual habits to a malevolent cosmos; and the Venus fly trap, the horror on the Encantadas, and Sebastian's final destruction are the play's three major symbols of a corrupt universe.

Williams has constructed a lofty framework in which to punish one of his sexual outlaws, while beneath the symbolic superstructure, he is really punishing his character for being a decadent homosexual. In its obscuring, overheated symbolism, in fact, and its veiled allusions to Sebastian's sexual agenda, the play is almost as evasive as *Cat on a Hot Tin Roof.* Both plays suggest that to be homosexual is to be desperately sick. Harold Clurman asked: "Why must all homosexuals in the theatre always be ascribed to the influence of over-possessive mothers, and why must homosexuals be effete? There are a great many vigorous and creative ones—in the world."[5] Patrick Dennis, also unhappy with the lavender tone of the play, complained, "there is just something *about* boys named Sebastian."[6]

But, characteristically, Williams has mixed feelings about his hero since there is exultation as well as revulsion in his depiction of Sebastian's death. For Williams, as Kenneth Tynan noted, "all aesthetes are sacred... the trouble is that we do not see him with Mr. Williams's eyes. . . . It is one thing to sympathize with a man who has been garrotted by the old umbilical cord. It is quite another when we are asked to see in his death (as Mr. Williams clearly wants us to) a modern re-enactment of the martyr-dom of St. Sebastian."[7] Williams may be uncomfortable in dramatizing Sebastian's sexual preferences, but he idealizes the character's self-created role as an artist whose "life was his work because the work of a poet is the life of a poet and—vice versa, the life of a poet is the work of a poet. I mean," says Violet Venable to Dr. Sugar, "you can't separate them . . . a poet's life is his work and his work is his life in a special sense." Williams says that, in *his* case, "a poet's work is his escape from his life,"[8] but Williams clearly celebrates Sebastian's aesthetic sensitivity. He wants us to admire the poet's dedication to art.

Despite its inflated imagery, its confused morality, and its flustered, shifty treatment of homosexuality, *Suddenly Last Summer* contains some of the playwright's most highly charged writing. Mrs. Venable's speech about the annihilation of the turtles and Catherine's final monologue which recounts the events leading up to Sebastian's death are virtuoso. As Kenneth Tynan commented, "'What a writer!' one murmurs during those passages. But one cannot honestly add: 'What a play!'"[9]

The play has especially vivid characters. Violet Venable is the ultimate Williams Gorgon; Catherine's witless, grasping mother and brother, and Miss Foxhill, Violet's squirrel-like secretary, are briskly rendered carica-tures. Only Dr. Sugar, who asks questions, and listens patiently, is a flat character. *Suddenly Last Summer* even has a solid story line, which is unusual for Williams. The play is built like a mystery, with our under-standing of the unmentionable events of last summer enlarged in enticing fragments. Dr. Sugar, as he probes, becomes less and less convinced of Catherine's insanity (indeed, as Signi Falk has written, she turns out to be "the rarest specimen in the entire literary jungle of Tennessee Williams: she is a normal human being"[10]); but her fate is uncertain until the end, and the play maintains the tension of a first-rate thriller.

Like *Cat on a Hot Tin Roof, Suddenly Last Summer* is a play about confession; but unlike Brick, Catherine is able to tell everything. Since Williams believes in the therapeutic value of confession, Catherine is cured, cleansed, once she is able to tell all, whereas Mrs. Venable, who never confronts the truth about her son, remains unpurged.

Telling the truth is crucial—and difficult—in Williams's play. In both this play and the earlier *Cat*, the characters' need to confess amounts to an obsession; but in both dramas Williams backs away from the underly-ing homosexual theme that is his real concern as well as the true focus of the confession motif. The full sexual identity of his heroes remains hidden beneath the gaudy and entertaining theatrical surface.

Catherine, who has nothing to lose and everything to gain by it, is the one character in *Suddenly Last Summer* who is capable of telling the truth. As Harold Clurman wrote, she is "a pure person who is victimized and confined to an insane asylum for daring to tell a truth abhorrent and inimical to the powers that be."[11] Williams perhaps used Catherine's incarceration as a metaphor for his own sense of himself as a renegade artist misunderstood by a hostile, disbelieving public. The play, at any rate, was the product of Williams's first period of psychoanalysis, and it is particularly rife with details from his own tortured psychological history. Signi Falk, one of the playwright's most unsparing critics, accused him of writing "another private and very sick view of the world. . . . Williams has carried his private symbolism to incredible extremes when he would make a decadent artist and aging homosexual . . . whose sexual perversion extended to younger and younger boys . . . a symbol to represent men of our times."[12]

Williams felt at the time of its production that

this violent and shocking [play was] in a sense a catharsis, a final fling of violence. . . . I think if this analysis works it will open some doors for me. . . . If I am no longer disturbed myself, I will deal less with disturbed people. . . . I think I have pretty well explored that aspect of life. . . . It would be good if I could write with serenity.[13]

Suddenly Last Summer is Williams's most high-strung, most baroque play, but it was not the catharsis he may have been hoping for. Unlike his heroine, he was not purged of visions of perversion and violence, and his following play is almost as morbid.

Sweet Bird of Youth is a Southern Gothic horror story in which a sexually errant male is both punished and deified. Chance Wayne is a gigolo who sells his body in exchange for promises of stardom. As his name blatantly indicates, though, his chances are waning; and at the awkward transitional age of thirty, he grasps with increasing desperation for the movie star fame that eludes him. When we first see him, he is in the middle of his most fevered scheme, playing the male nurse to a fading actress, and prepared to blackmail her (for possession of hashish) into pushing him and his girlfriend into the movies.

Chance is one of Williams's desperate dreamers, a good-looking small town boy whose ambitions exceed his talent. Like many Williams characters, he is trying to hold on to the fleeting "sweet bird of youth." Traveling with aging prima donna Alexandra del Lago, Chance returns to his home town of Saint Cloud expecting to find it exactly as he left it. He soon learns that the memory of his former glories has dimmed. His mother has died, his girl's father won't let him see her; Chance returns home a fallen hero, and like Val Xavier in *Battle of Angels,* he is pursued and finally destroyed by the town rednecks. Chance's emphatic sexual presence is a threat to the men of the town, and like Val, Chance is regarded as a diseased intruder who must be expelled in order to insure the health of the community.

The character is so beleaguered that he himself comes to think that he deserves his awful fate, offering himself to his pursuers as a kind of sacrificial victim. Immediately before he is castrated by them, he speaks directly to the audience: "I don't ask for your pity, but just for your understanding—not even that—no. Just for your recognition of me in you, and the enemy, time, in us all." Many critics were puzzled by the character's request, for Chance is not convincing as an Everyman. Robert Brustein charged:

Since Chance has had about as much universality as a character in an animated cartoon, to regard his experience as an illuminating reflection of the human condition is a notion which borders on the grotesque. For *Sweet Bird of Youth* is a highly private neurotic fantasy which takes place in a Terra Incognita quite remote from the terrain of the waking world.[14]

Williams treats his Adonis as both the purest and the most depraved character in the play. Chance is both childlike innocent and tortured self-flagellant, both pagan sensualist and Christian sinner. He laments the loss of the innocence he had when he and his girl Heavenly were young, unashamed lovers; and yet he celebrates his vocation ("maybe the only one I was truly meant for") as a professional lover: "I gave people more than I took. Middle-aged people I gave back a feeling of youth. Lonely girls? Understanding, appreciation! An absolutely convincing show of affection. Sad people, lost people? Something light and uplifting! Eccentrics? Tolerance, even odd things they long for." Though he is self-loathing at times, Chance nonetheless feels he is superior to Heavenly's dictatorial father Boss Finley: "He was just called down from the hills to preach hate. I was born here to make love."

Chance, then, is both healer and destroyer; his body soothes the lonely and the no longer young just as it has infected Heavenly, for Chance is an Adonis who spreads venereal disease. (As Kenneth Tynan noted: "None of Mr. Williams's other plays has contained so much rot. It is as if the author were hypnotized by his subject, like a rabbit by a snake, or a Puritan by sin."[15])

Chance is guilty because he has robbed Heavenly of her innocence and her womanhood (she has had to have a hysterectomy as a result of the disease Chance passed on to her) and because he has squandered his own youth on a succession of one-night stands with strangers. He regards his punishment as only just, and the courage he shows in the face of catastrophe is clearly meant to vindicate him. As John Hays has written, he "ironically gains in manliness at the moment he faces the loss of his manhood."[16] Chance is cleansed by willfully surrendering himself to castration. The play thus equates castration with resurrection—"a very personal and psychological resurrection," as Hays notes, rather than "the spring-time renewal of fortune Adonis was credited with."[17]

Typically for Williams, as Arthur Ganz has suggested, it is only after the character "has been punished and destroyed [that he can] be revered."[18] The punishment, though, is not consistent with Williams's celebration of Chance as a healer and restorer. Robert Brustein pointed out the contradiction: "The bird not only represents purity but . . . the male sexual organ. If the bird is a phallic image, then Chance's sweetness and youth are associated with sexuality . . . and his purity is terminated only when he is castrated, not when he turns to more perverse pleasures."[19]

Chance is both Christ crucified for our sins (as the final speech makes clear) and Adonis, the unashamed, joy-creating god of fertility.[20] Williams's play is both Christian fable and pagan myth. The play's unresolved conflicts are derived from the author's private neuroses, but he is showman enough to convert his personal obsessions into exciting melodrama. Although Williams tries to give the story religious significance, at heart *Sweet Bird of Youth* is a glossy shocker about sex and politics.

The hero may be the protagonist of both a popular romance and a symbolic religious pageant, but the play's two supporting characters, Alexandra del Lago and Boss Finley, are rooted firmly on the level of garish melodrama. Alexandra is such a rich character part that it is possible to overlook the fact that she is incidental to both the story and theme.

Her try for a comeback, we learn, was disastrous because Alexandra del Lago at forty-seven has too many wrinkles to attempt the kinds of parts that made her a star when she was young. As she enters the play, she's on the run from her unsuccessful new career, and she's determined to forget failure through hashish and Chance. But improbably, Alexandra finds out that her comeback was not the fiasco she has imagined it was, and she is once again a star. In a flash, she forgets her promises to Chance, and she is on her way back to Hollywood. Williams elaborates the actress's role in the play much more than he needs to. Aside from eliciting his life story from Chance, Alexandra is necessary only as a thematic reinforcement of Chance's lust for success and his fear of growing older. Both characters regard time as the enemy; the actress "knew in her heart that the legend of Alexandra del Lago couldn't be separated from an appearance of youth." Aware of the corruption of these two characters, Williams nevertheless sympathizes with them; typically, he wants both to punish them and to save them.

His feelings about Boss Finley are much less complicated. Williams claims he was unsuccessful with Finley because he hated him so much: "I have to understand the characters in my play. . . . If I just hate them I can't write about them. That's why Boss Finley wasn't right . . . because I just didn't like the guy, and I just had to make a tour de force of his part in the play."[21] But like Alexandra, Boss Finley is a wonderfully outgoing character. He is a backwoods politician who savors his power; and he is a fraud who is used to having his own way. He forces his defiled daughter Heavenly to stand before his constituents as a symbol of virginal Southern maidenhood. The old man resembles Chance in thinking of himself as a healer: "I have told you before, but I will tell you again. I got a mission that I hold sacred to perform in the Southland. . . . When I was fifteen I came down barefooted out of the red clay hills. . . . And what is this mission? . . . To shield from pollution a blood that I think is not only sacred to me, but sacred to Him." Williams uses Hollywood glamor and Southern bigotry as tokens of universal corruption, but his treatment of movies and politics as tainted pursuits is too sketchy to serve a serious symbolic function.

Sweet Bird of Youth is tawdry and carelessly constructed. The first two acts have little connection to each other as the action moves disjointedly from Chance and Alexandra to Boss Finley; act 2 ends with a chaotically dramatized political rally; and in act 3, the destinies of Chance and Alexandra are uneasily integrated. But the play has vitality, and this gaudy story of movie stars and Southern demagogues is absorbing on a superficial level.

6

TWO "AFFIRMATIVE" PLAYS

Williams's two plays written in the early sixties, *Period of Adjustment* and *The Night of the Iguana,* are guardedly, almost reluctantly optimistic. The characters in both plays have happy fates: husbands are reunited with wives; an old poet completes his final, long-awaited poem; a defrocked minister is comforted by his fiery mistress. They are as haunted and as sexually obsessed as the characters in earlier plays, but they survive. In these muted, and at least tentatively affirmative dramas, there are no lynchings or castrations or cannibalistic dismemberments—the characters are not punished for their sexual misconduct.

If *Suddenly Last Summer* resulted from the early period of Williams's therapy, *Period of Adjustment* and *The Night of the Iguana* represent the effects of longer-range analysis: "I suppose with psychoanalysis," Williams said when *Period of Adjustment* was produced, "comes some measure of adjustment. . . . Not that I'm any happier. I think I'm even less happy with this new self-knowledge, but there is no longer the desperation. I don't take things so seriously. I don't pity myself or beat my breast."[1]

Period of Adjustment was announced, as *The Rose Tattoo* had been a decade before, as something new for Williams. It was advertised as a domestic comedy and audiences were led to expect a lightweight offering in the manner of Neil Simon. Williams spoke about the play in a casual tone, as if it were merely an occasional piece: "It's an unambitious play. I only wanted to tell the truth about a little occurrence in life, without blowing it up beyond its natural limits";[2] "this was a very impersonal play. I usually identify with the characters . . . but this was different."[3]

The play, however, which considers the "period of adjustment" in two shaky marriages, is not as relaxed or as genial as Williams and his producers had hoped it would be, since the characters are all sexual misfits. George shakes uncontrollably at the prospect of sex. His new bride Isabel is a sheltered daddy's girl who is also terrified of sex. Ralph has trouble making love to Dorothy because he finds her so unattractive; and Dorothy has been frigid because she has always been aware of her homeliness. These four characters are not promising candidates for a commercial marital comedy, and Williams realized the play's gloomy underpinning only after he had completed it: "I had the impression that this was a happy play, but when I saw it this summer in the stock production with Dane Clark, I realized that it was about as black as *Orpheus Descending,* except that there was more tenderness."[4]

Although the remorseful, guilt-ridden couples are reconciled, the conventional upbeat finale is not convincing. "If you analyze it carefully," Williams noted, "it hasn't really a happy ending. It's only happy in the sense that all the characters are alive and that they are interested in going on living. This is about as far as I could go with that Pollyanna stuff."[5]

Period of Adjustment is Williams's only play with a conventional middle-class setting. Nowhere else in the canon is there so much attention to interior decoration, household appliances, jobs, and children's toys. For the play's two couples, as for few other Williams characters, the center of life is marriage and the family. The characters may not be normal according to the standards of Broadway domestic comedy, but they are relatively sane compared to the people in Williams's other plays.

Ralph and George are former Army buddies who feel they have failed. Ralph married Dorothy because she has a rich, ailing father, but he is trapped in a low-paying desk job. George is a self-advertised ladies' man who is really afraid of women, being much more comfortable in masculine company, where he can boast of his conquests. Like the characters in *Death of a Salesman,* George and Ralph have the wrong dreams. Because they have accepted the values of their conservative Southern society, they feel obligated to have pretty wives, important jobs, and impressive houses, though they are almost as uncomfortable with middle-class ideals as the rest of Williams's characters are. They are romantics who would be happiest outside the Establishment, and for a moment, they entertain a vision of escape. They have a plan for a rural life far removed from plastic suburbia—George wants to raise cattle and buffalo in Texas, for Western movies. The friends are charmed by the notion of comradeship in a rugged, womanless America. For George, especially, the vision is soothing because it offers an escape from his new, feared wife; and for Ralph, too, the country life provides a refuge from his dull factory job and from the unenticing wife who is turning their three-year-old boy into a sissy.

Their reconciliations with their wives at the end of the play are not believable because it is clear that George and Ralph would be happier together. Despite their display of ruggedness, George and Ralph are terrified of the masculine roles their society expects them to fulfill. They do not want to sleep with women. George is afraid of Isabel simply because she is a woman, and he does not want to risk being ridiculed by failing with her in bed; and Ralph is repelled by his wife's plainness. In its own quiet way, *Period of Adjustment*, like *Cat on a Hot Tin Roof*, is a play about indoctrination into heterosexuality.

The wives are as uncertain as their husbands of their own sexual identities. Dorothy is so insecure that she had plastic surgery in order to be more appealing to Ralph. And Isabel, a nurse who enticed George with her expert massages, is in fact a virgin. She is one of Williams's sweet, forlorn women, and she anticipates the character of Myrtle in *Kingdom of Earth* because, like Myrtle, she is a nervous, non-stop talker who manages to place herself in humiliating circumstances. On only the second night of her marriage, she is jobless and temporarily abandoned by her husband.

These four helpless, likable characters resist Williams's attempts to turn them into ordinary married couples. Williams, finally, is not a persuasive spokesman for the joys of marriage and the family, and the play's main symbol reveals his true attitude to the subject. The play is subtitled "High Point over a Cavern" because the tract house that the Bateses live in is slipping gradually into a subterranean pit. Marriage, tract house, supermarkets, TV dinners, up-to-the-minute appliances are not firmly grounded; the world that the play sets up is destined to be consumed by the underlying vacuum.

Williams's evident distaste for the suburban, middle-class way of life clashes with his determination to give the play an upbeat ending. The characters are outsiders, finally, too odd and too scared to qualify as average husbands and wives and parents. *Period of Adjustment* is as close to typical middle-class comedy as Williams is ever likely to get, and the strain shows.

The Night of the Iguana is also wary in its affirmations, though the characters are released from their demons in a more persuasive way than in the preceding play. Williams has said that his theme in this drama is "how to live beyond despair and still live."[6]

The characters are a defrocked minister who conducts tours for Southern schoolgirls through the Mexican jungles; a ninety-seven-year-old aesthete, the world's oldest living practicing poet; his spinster granddaughter; and the blowsy middle-aged proprietress at the dilapidated pension where the characters converge. Though they are often deeply troubled as the drama develops, the characters are at peace at the end. The poet, at long last, completes his poem; the spinster travels on alone, her spirit untarnished; the minister has found refuge at the inn; and the proprietress has the minister.

An iguana, caught by native boys and tied to a tree under the verandah on which the action takes place, is the play's blatant symbol. Like the sinking house built over a cavern in *Period of Adjustment,* the tied iguana is a constant reminder of the play's theme. Williams said at the time of the play's production, "Yes, the iguana is a symbol. . . . We're trying to play it cool so it doesn't become too symbolic. . . . It doesn't stand for any particular character in the play, perhaps it stands for the human situation."[7] The bound and wriggling iguana reinforces the fact that the characters suffer; and the iguana's release at the end of the play signifies the characters' liberation.

Reverend T. Lawrence Shannon, excommunicated for heresy and fornication, dedicates himself to "the gospel of God as Lightning and Thunder." But Shannon is not equal to his ideal of a rapacious and vengeful God because he is merely an overaged delinquent who rebels against a conservative family background and a tame middle-class concept of God. Maxine, the hotel owner, reminds Shannon that when his mother caught him practicing "the little boy's vice,"

she had to punish you for it because it made God mad as much as it did Mama. . . . You said you loved God and Mama and so you quit it to please them, but it was your secret pleasure and you harbored a secret resentment against Mama and God for making you give it up. And so you got back at God by preaching atheistical sermons and you got back at Mama by starting to lay young girls.

Shannon is like a misbehaving child who delights in shocking the philistines. From preaching about a God of Thunder and Lightning to a congregation weaned on a concept of God as "a bad-tempered, childish, old, old, sick, peevish man," he descends to conducting irregular tours to "the underworlds of all places." Like the playwright himself, Shannon celebrates oddity and perversion, taking his ladies to places they have never seen or even imagined. Harold Clurman suggested that we must "perceive the drift of *Iguana* in its relation to its author's legend. . . . Shannon is an outcast, bringing to his tourists' attention the secret and foul byways of man's experience."[8] Shannon leads his tourists to places that expand their vision: "The whole world . . . God's world, has been the range of my travels," Shannon advertises. "I haven't stuck to the schedules of the brochures, and I've always allowed the ones that were willing to see, to *see* . . . and if they had hearts to be touched, feelings to feel with, I gave them a priceless chance to feel and be touched. And none will ever forget it." But now, on this tour, Shannon has failed to capture the imaginations of his group; his "artistry" has reached only the shallow, pretty Charlotte. Jealous of his hold over Charlotte, Miss Fellowes, the lesbian vocal coach of a Baptist College in Texas, accuses Shannon of being a lecher and a fraud and she sets out with manic determination to wreck him.

A failed man of God, now faced with failure as a guide of the underworld, Shannon has arrived at Maxine's hotel in order to collapse. Though he tries to disguise his guilt by playing the angry rebel, Shannon is one of Williams's walking wounded. In flight from his mother, he yet needs a mother to comfort him, and his salvation is with the middle-aged, hot-blooded earth mother Maxine.

Shannon is similar to many Williams heroes in holding a special fascination for women, but he is not very fond of most of them: "Women, whether they face it or not, want to see a man in a tied-up situation. They work at it all their lives, to get a man in a tied-up situation. Their lives are fulfilled, they're satisfied at last, when they get a man, or as many men as they can, in the tied-up situation." Though he is suspicious of them, Shannon (unlike some of Williams's males) nevertheless needs women. Maxine, and Hannah Jelkes, a New England spinster, release Shannon from the "spook" that bedevils him: this situation of a troubled male soothed by women is unique in the Williams canon. Maxine and Hannah are both mother figures, and yet (also unusual for Williams) they are presented as saviors rather than destroyers.

Shannon stays with Maxine because, as Maxine says, "we've both reached a point where we've got to settle for something that works for us in our lives—even if it isn't on the highest kind of level." In a different way, Shannon and Hannah are good for each other too. Hannah is the fair heroine, the saint, to Maxine's whore. She is a prim Williams matron, but unlike Alma Winemiller in *Summer and Smoke*, she is not a hysteric. She is not tormented by conflicting claims of spirit and flesh. Traveling with her grandfather through the tourist places of the world and selling her paintings as he recites his poetry, she calmly accepts her fate; in the face of poverty and dependence on the kindness of strangers, she never falters. Hannah is one of Williams's few absolutely poised characters.

The act 2 dialogue between Shannon, tied up in a hammock following a tantrum, and Hannah, a ministering angel, is a kind of earthly communion. Hannah's serenity calms the tormented Reverend, while his earthiness relaxes her. Hannah sees through what she calls Shannon's "Passion Play performance," and she knows that he is uneasy with his self-appointed roles of atheist and seducer. Their generosity to each other contains the play's main theme:

Hannah: Liquor isn't your problem, Mr. Shannon.
Shannon: What is my problem, Miss Jelkes?
Hannah: The oldest one in the world—the need to believe in something or in someone. . .
Shannon: Something like . . . God?
Hannah: No.
Shannon: What?
Hannah: Broken gates between people so they can reach each other, even if it's just for one night only.
Shannon: One night stands, huh?
Hannah: One night communication between them on a verandah outside their separate cubicles.

Together, the defrocked Reverend and the New England spinster get beyond "subterranean travels, the . . . journeys that the spooked and bedeviled people are forced to take through the . . . the *unlighted* sides of their natures." Hannah continues alone on her travels while Shannon remains with Maxine, but for this one night, Flesh and Spirit joined together.

Williams based the play on his own "salvation" in Mexico twenty years before:

It was then that I discovered it was not only life that I truly longed for, but that [that] which is most valuable in life is escaping from the narrow cubicle of one's self to a sort of verandah between the sky and the still-water beach (allegorically speaking) and to a hammock beside another beleaguered being, someone else who is in exile from the place and time of his heart's fulfillment.... The alternative title, *Two Acts of Grace* ... referred to a pair of desperate people who had the humble nobility of each putting the other's desperation, during the course of a night, above his own. Being an unregenerate romanticist, even now I can still think of nothing that gives more meaning to life.[9]

The release of the iguana and the cleansing confessions of Hannah and Shannon are matched by Nonno's completion of his poem. The poem mingles Williams's preoccupations with death ("A bargaining with mist and mould") and corruption ("the earth's obscene, corrupting love") with praise of courage and endurance:

> How calmly does the orange branch
> Observe the sky begin to blanch
> Without a cry, without a prayer,
> With no betrayal of despair.
>
> O Courage, could you, not as well
> Select a second place to dwell,
> Not only in that golden tree
> But in the frightened heart of me?

The poem, like the play itself, transforms into a song of praise the playwright's recurrent fears of loss of youth and the passing of time. Joy triumphs over death and disfigurement. The tree's "broken stem" and inevitable "plummeting to earth" are challenged:

> And still the ripe fruit and the branch
> Observe the sky begin to blanch
> Without a cry, without a prayer,
> With no betrayal of despair.

The Night of the Iguana, then, dramatizes Williams's belief in the transforming and healing powers of art and of confession, for Nonno's poem, like the confessions of the other characters, is therapeutic. The old man dies, his life resolved through the ordering of art while Shannon and Hannah are restored by their one-night communion.

The play contains Williams's least sensational treatment of his perennial theme of the conflict between flesh and spirit. The drama still depends on the collision of sexual types—the lady and the whore, the sensual man and the repressed woman—but the characters are comfortable with their sexual natures. Maxine and Hannah embody, individually, traits that are combined in tortured, schizophrenic characters like Blanche Du Bois and Alma Winemiller; the simplification of the characters' sexuality gives the play its mellow tone. Bette Davis, who originated the role of Maxine, commented that the character "is basically an animal, a good healthy animal. She wants one thing, guys, and this guy in particular.... She is not two-sided, like most Williams characters. She's fairly direct, down-to-earth, uncomplicated."[10] She is not, in short, a Williams caricature.

Hannah and Shannon are also freshly observed. Williams does not treat Hannah as a stereotypical spinster, but instead presents her as radiant and wise—she is probably his purest character. For a change too, it is the man in this play who is more neurotic than the women. Shannon, who is a poseur, a self-dramatizer, is something of a straight male version of Blanche Du Bois, though unlike Blanche, he finds protection.

Typical of Williams's confession dramas, the play is basically a series of monologues: Shannon on the nature of God; Hannah on art; Maxine on sex.[11] Since it has less of a traditional story line than any of the earlier plays, *Iguana* looks forward to such confession dramas as *In the Bar of a Tokyo Hotel* and *Small-Craft Warnings.* There is, in fact, too much discussion in the play. Characteristically, Williams strains to place his people in a cosmic frame, and the drama is embroidered with speeches about God and art and with discussions of life as a mixture of the sun and the shadow, the realistic and the fantastic. The barbarous German family that Williams brings on throughout the action is extraneous, though the playwright has argued that "they offer a vivid counterpoint—as world conquerors—to the world-conquered protagonists of the play.... In a way they correspond to Stanley Kowalski in *Streetcar.* Instead of one Blanche Du Bois, I have three."[12] But Stanley is a full-bodied character as well as a symbol, whereas the oafish Germans exist only on the symbolic level. *The Night of the Iguana* is a strong character study that doesn't need its religious and philosophical embellishments: the problems of the characters don't need to be seen with respect to the problems of mankind.

7

PORTRAITS OF THE
PLAYWRIGHT AS FAILURE

The Night of the Iguana was Williams's last popular success to date. The first production of *The Milk Train Doesn't Stop Here Any More*, in 1962, is commonly regarded as the beginning of his slump, and whether off-Broadway, in London, or Chicago, his work since then has met with diminishing popular and critical acceptance. Critics have sometimes cruelly relegated him to the position of an old-fashioned, sentimental playwright, and during this time, Williams was accused more than ever of self-parody.

Williams himself has said recently that during much of the sixties, as he battled drugs and alcohol and recurrent periods of depression, he was lost to the world; in 1969, he was placed in a mental hospital. The plays written during this unhappy time naturally reflect the strain: *The Milk Train Doesn't Stop Here Any More, Slapstick Tragedy* (1966), *In the Bar of a Tokyo Hotel* (1969), *Small-Craft Warnings,* and *Out Cry* (1973) are decidedly minor works. Only one play of this period, *Kingdom of Earth* (1968), is first-rate Williams, but it too failed to attract critics and audiences.

With the exceptions of *Small-Craft Warnings* and *Kingdom of Earth,* these plays are about failed artists. Flailing, hounded, mocked, unable to separate art from life, reduced to bizarre and spectacular failure, working frantically against time, the artists of the plays are clearly the repositories for the playwright's own despair; Williams was sending out notes from his own underground. In these dramas Williams exposed his famous problems in more direct ways than he ever had before. As Harold Clurman wrote about *In the Bar of a Tokyo Hotel,* "there are things which an artist feels he *must* deliver himself of, no matter how 'tasteless' the display may appear to his friends and critics. Without this release and purgation, such an artist may feel unable to proceed and renew himself."[1]

In these thinly disguised self-portraits, Williams is writing more to explore his own problems than to entertain audiences. Private, intensely egocentric, these are chamber plays that chart the playwright's own insecurities. Trying for new ways of relating to his work and to his audience, Williams no longer thought of himself as a popular writer but as a tortured spirit in search of self-understanding.

In *The Milk Train Doesn't Stop Here Any More,* a jet set celebrity who was once a famous Follies girl and "a legend in her own lifetime," is dying alone in her mountaintop villa, shrieking her memoirs into a tape recorder while her publisher's deadlines bring on "a sort of nervous breakdown." Williams's sixties plays are the equivalent of this character's fevered autobiography.

The Gnadiges Fraulein, the title character in one of the two short plays that comprise *Slapstick Tragedy,* is even more desperate and more grotesque than Flora Goforth in *Milk Train.* A once-renowned circus celebrity, she is reduced to competing with the Cockaloony Bird for fish for her supper. In *In the Bar of a Tokyo Hotel,* the painter, dazed by his work, kills himself. In *Out Cry,* a brother and sister, members of a theatrical troupe, are stranded in a cold, abandoned theater. These characters all suggest Williams's struggles with his sense of failure.

These are not easy plays to warm to since Williams does not court our approval in the way that he did with his work of the fifties. These plays, which avoid conventional narrative structure even more than is customary for Williams, are the most experimental and the most difficult in the canon. With its Kabuki stagehands and abstract setting, *Milk Train* tries for Brechtian detachment. *The Gnadiges Fraulein* is conceived as a knockabout vaudeville routine—Ionesco crossed with the Keystone Cops. *Tokyo Hotel* and *Out Cry* are introverted plays, "tone poems," that explore the playwright's continuing concern with the relationship between his life and his art. These sad, uncommercial plays are the most personal works of a notoriously self-involved writer.

Like *Battle of Angels, The Milk Train Doesn't Stop Here Any More* is one of those plays that Williams could not let go of. He rewrote it three times. It was produced on Broadway for the first time in 1962, and it was presented in a revised version the following season. "*Milk Train* was the most frustrating experience I've ever been through," Williams said. "It was never a successful piece of work. . . . I keep rewriting it all the time, but I've never gotten it right . . . the part of the boy was never realized."[2] As late as the summer of 1972, Williams was still reworking the play—this time for Angela Lansbury and Michael York, "though they don't know it yet, poor dears."[3]

Milk Train is yet another variation on the archetypal Williams fable—the interaction between a muscled young man and an aging woman. Robert Brustein suggested that the play was "Williams's four-hundred-thirty-fourth version of the encounter between a pure-corrupt young man and an ogrish, corrupting older woman in a lush and fruity setting."[4] The play resembles especially the design of Williams's novel, *The Roman Spring of Mrs. Stone,* in which an imperious, declining celebrity is attracted to and challenged by a princely male hustler. As in that earlier version of the encounter, Williams regards his fading beauty with a mixture of amusement, camaraderie, and contempt, and looks at the peacock male with both awe and disapproval.

Yet in the play Williams tries more than ever before to give this familiar confrontation the stature of moral allegory. He tries to place his rapacious woman and his prize male in a context of mystic transcendence. The play, as Richard Gilman noted, is a "quest" for "a way out of the impasse created by a belief in the redemptive nature of sexual efficacy."[5] At the same time, then, that Williams dwells on his characters' physical traits— the strapping hero, the disintegrating heroine—he is intent on writing a play about ways of transcending the claims of the flesh: Flora Goforth is saved because, for once, a man refuses to enter her bedroom. The hero, too, is a savior because he will not sleep with his hostess. The play thus presents the curious spectacle of a meeting between a desirable man and a woman world-famous for her sexual excesses that celebrates the sanctity of denial. The characters don't fit the theme: Flora is too strident and earthy and Chris reeks of Forty-second Street—these Bohemian types do not convincingly indicate the joys of celibacy.

Boisterous, clown-like Flora has secluded herself in a fortressed villa on a hilltop in Capri in order to record her memories of scandalous and foolish escapades. Williams has said that Flora is based on Tallulah Bank-head, and the portrait is not flattering. The character has bravado, but she is tiresomely self-indulgent, petulant, and demanding. A sexually voracious gossip who is haughty to her employees and to her guests, Flora is the ultimate Williams transvestite. With her sleazy camp sensibility and her litany of endless gripes, she is one of his most unpleasant characters. As Harold Clurman wrote, "The portrait is harshly comic; more like catty caricature and gossip than honest delineation. . . . The laughter it provokes . . . is not kindly or understanding. The observation evident in the portrayal may be sharply accurate but its spirit is unwholesomely derisive."[6].

The scene between Flora and her friend The Witch of Capri typifies the play's arch tone. Williams is eavesdropping on the shallow jet set, and though he caricatures them, he seems trapped in an unwholesome, almost sycophantic relationship to Flora and her ilk.

The Witch:	Do we have to eat?—I'm so full of canapes from Mona's cocktail do . . .
Mrs. Goforth:	Oh, is that what you're full of? . . . what's your latest name, Connie?
The Witch:	I mailed you my wedding invitation the spring before last spring to some hospital in Boston, the Leahey Clinic, and never received a word of acknowledgment from you. . . .
Mrs. Goforth:	—Are you still living on blood transfusions, Connie? That's not good, it turns you into a vampire, a pipis-trella, ha ha. . . . Your neck's getting too thin, Connie. Is it true you had the sheep embryo-plantation in Switzerland? I heard so: don't approve of it. It keys you up for a while and then you collapse, completely. The human system can't stand too much stimulation after—sixty. . . .
The Witch:	When you called me today I was so relieved I could die: shouted "Hallelujah" silently, to myself. I'd heard such distressing rumors about you lately, Sissy.
Mrs. Goforth:	Rumors? Hell, what rumors?
The Witch:	I can't tell you the rumors that have been circulating about you since your houseparty last month. The ones you brought over from Capri came back to Capri with stories I love you too much to repeat.

Flora goes on in this brittle, affected manner for the entire play, her acid wit punctuated with hacking coughs. As Williams presents her, "Sissy" Goforth seems like the Mother Superior of Camp. The bitchy dialogue is often amusing, but it does not serve Williams's ambitious theme.

In his program note, Williams wrote that the play is intended to speak to our fears of death: "In *Milk Train* I am trying once more to make a tragedy in which the protagonist is not a human being but a universal condition of human beings ... the apparently incomprehensible but surely somehow significant adventure of being alive that we all must pass through for a time." Yet as an Everyman figure Flora is no more appropriate than Chance Wayne in *Sweet Bird of Youth* because, like Chance, she is a colorful caricature derived from the playwright's purely private fantasies. Williams distorts the play in attempting to give this "death of a clown" metaphysical dimension. Aware of the disparity between the form of the play and its content, Williams asked audiences not to think of him as "a cold and brutal writer" who treats "the subject of dying in a style that is often comic.... I hope ... that you will be reminded that death comes to clowns as well as to kings and heroes." Williams does not like Flora ("there is hardly a bit of nobility, nor even of dignity, in her fiercely resistant approach to life's most awful adventure"), yet he wants us "to pity this female clown even while her absurd pretensions and her panicky last effort to hide from her final destruction make [us] laugh at her." Sissy Goforth, who is convincing as a madcap drag queen on holiday, is not convincing as anything more exalted.

Isolated in her glamorous hilltop villa and dictating her memoirs at chaotic speed to a level-headed and disapproving secretary, Flora is a fighter who insists that she will not "go forth" this summer. The omens are bad, however, when a young man, a poet named Christopher Flanders, breaks his way into her barricaded compound. Chris has a Mediterranean-wide reputation for visiting dying rich ladies and for helping to ease their transition from life to death.

Williams rewrote this dance of death between a shrill ex-burlesque queen and a blond young mystic because he wanted "to make the male character ... more balanced with the female."[7] Williams said that Chris is "a truly pure person ... who makes Flora realize that she is not as hard a bitch as she imagines."[8] He developed the character after a trip to the Orient left him "deeply impressed with Eastern philosophy." Blond and fair, Chris brings Flora "values that her life was the opposite of."[9] He is the bringer of light, yet all he receives from his hostess is black coffee because, as she tells him, the milk train doesn't stop any more at her place. A wanderer, a philosopher, a maker of mobiles, a sometime poet, Chris is magnetically good-looking. The rich old women he visits want to sleep with him, but he remains celibate; he is their asexual guardian angel who leads them calmly to death.

In one of the play's vivid set speeches, Chris explains how he discovered his vocation.

I stopped for a swim off the beach that was completely deserted, swam out in the cool water till my head felt cool as the water: then turned and swam back in, but the beach wasn't deserted completely any longer. There was a very old gentleman on it. He called "Help!" to me, as if he was in the water, drowning, and I was on shore. I swam in and asked him how I could help him and he said this, he said: "Help me out there, I can't make it alone, I've gone past pain I can bear."—I could see it was true. He was elegantly dressed but emaciated, cadaverous. I gave him the help he wanted, I led him out in the water, it wasn't easy. Once he started to panic, I had to hold on to him tight as a lover till he got back his courage and said, all right, the tide took him as light as a leaf. But just before I did that, and this is the oddest thing, he took out his wallet and thrust all the money in it into my hand. Here take this, he said to me. And I—The sea had no use for his money. The fish in the sea had no use for it either, so I took it and went on where I was going.

As Chris describes it, the encounter with the old man suggests a bargain between an elderly homosexual and a young hustler. A sexual contract is transformed into a mystical transaction, with the hustler as a priest who administers his own special version of the last rites.

Chris, then, represents a curious mixture of the flesh-spirit conflict that underlies all of Williams's work. Like Alma Winemiller, who moves from the minister's cloister to the town square, and like Val Xavier, who has been on a party and now wants to devote himself to the contemplative life, Chris is both intensely sexual and strangely ethereal. Guiding foolish, obscene old women to their deaths, he is at once a figure of sexuality, mortality, and deliverance. His presence excites the old women he visits, but it also notifies them that their time is up. For his hostesses, he represents finality as well as release.

This play which is obsessed by death detained Williams throughout his breakdown period. Doubtless Williams identified with Flora, a once-famous performer who draws frantically on her exhausted resources; but the play was important to Williams too because it is the most ambitious treatment of his recurrent older woman–young gigolo theme. When he rewrote it, Williams tried to emphasize the play's religious base by surrounding the characters with theatrical trimmings borrowed from nonrealistic dramatic styles. He added "a pair of stage assistants that function in a way that's between the Kabuki Theatre of Japan and the chorus of Greek theatre. My excuse, or reason, is that I think the play will come off better the further it is removed from conventional theatre since it's been rightly described as an allegory."[10]

The Milk Train Doesn't Stop Here Any More is Williams's final and most baroque version to date of his favorite subject. The sixties plays that follow it avoid the prototypical old woman–young man contretemps and concentrate instead on failed artists.

The Mutilated—"a play about cancer"—and *The Gnadiges Fraulein*— "a play about terrible birds"—were presented together under the title *Slapstick Tragedy*. In both short works Williams tries for new ways to handle familiar themes. "Vaudeville, burlesque, and slapstick, with a dash of pop art thrown in" (as Williams describes them), the theatrical surfaces of the two plays cannot disguise the fact that once again Williams is concerned with lost, wounded people. Williams describes the plays as "fantastic allegories on the tragicomic subject of human experience on this risky planet," and therefore, in both style and theme, they represent elaborations of the kind of fantasy drama Williams was moving toward in *The Milk Train Doesn't Stop Here Any More.* The two short pieces are freakshows that Williams has called "a bit like the feature stories in that newspaper, *The National Enquirer* . . . the finest journalistic review of the precise time that we live in."[11] "I don't think they'll work," Williams predicted gloomily before the plays opened. "*Slapstick Tragedy* is in the same vein as *Camino Real,* and *Camino Real* didn't go over well."[12]

Both dramas are about persistence and salvation. Trinket, the heroine of *The Mutilated,* is another of Williams's dispossessed characters; she has had a mastectomy, and the other transients at her hotel mock her for her "mutilation." But she and her friend Celeste are calmed when they have a vision of Our Lady. The Gnadiges Fraulein, another of the world's mutilated and one of the playwright's most grotesque characters, also receives grace. Like Flora Goforth, the Fraulein was once an international celebrity; she performed in a trained seal act. But now, in her decline, she is forced to earn her living by competing with the Cockaloony Bird for the fishermen's daily leftovers. The Fraulein is thus the most pathetic, and the most bizarre, of Williams's doomed artists.

The character is scorned, battle-scarred, accustomed to humiliation (the seal-trainer she worked with in her heyday constantly ridiculed her); yet each day she prepares for her encounter with the Cockaloony Bird as if she were still entertaining the crowned heads of Europe. She is gradually losing her faculties (her hearing is gone, and by the end of the play both her eyes are gouged out), but she survives.

Williams's own pain lurks beneath the play's zany, far-fetched situation. Here in this fanciful absurdist comedy the playwright is dealing with some of his most deeply felt themes: the humiliations of age, the loss of fame, the drying up of artistic power. Like several other sixties plays, *The Gnadiges Fraulein* reflects Williams's fears of having passed his prime.

The Fraulein is the most unusual version of Williams's fading actress archetype. She is one of his self-abasing characters; her catty landlady talks about how shabbily the seal-trainer treated her: "A Viennese dandy? Elegant? Youthful? Ravishingly attractive? Hapsburg crest on the signet ring on his pinkie? What could he throw to the Gnadiges Fraulein but an insincere smile with a very slight insincere bow that broke her heart every time she received it from him? He couldn't stand her because she adored him." To get the trainer's attention, the Fraulein began to compete with the seal, and her act of debasement became an international sensation. But on one occasion "the seal turned on her and fetched her such a terrific CLOUT!—Left flipper, right flipper—To her delicate jawbone that her pearly whites flew from her mouth like popcorn out of a popper. Honest to Gosh, sprayed out of her choppers like foam from a wild wave, breaking! They rang down the curtain.—The act was quickly disbanded." Losing her "sense of reality," the Fraulein began to drift—she just "drifted *and* drifted and *drifted.* . . ."

Prostrating herself before the handsome, scornful man she worships, the Fraulein is one of Williams's born victims. The details of her wretched career are plainly fantastic; her suffering, however, is real. Humiliated before thousands, spurned by the man she loves, and rejected, finally, by her public, the Fraulein is Williams's most garishly presented failure.

The bright, fanciful set, the low comedy supporting characters, the vaudeville pace, and the dazzling comic monologues may indicate that Williams is in a lighthearted mood, that he has written an entertainment, a sprightly stylistic exercise (Williams called the play "a diversion . . . done with little thought of anything but self-amusement and relief from the long, long haul of making a full-length play"[13]), but *The Gnadiges Fraulein* is not a lark. The playwright's own suffering gives the play a shrill, strained quality that made critics and audiences uncomfortable. Harold Clurman wrote that the play "is filled with sardonic mirth at the plight of the artist applauded and glamorized in his triumphs and then repudiated and derided when he fails. . . . He attempts to ward off self-pity through self-mockery, avenging himself on the 'enemy' with satiric lunacy. . . . I could not bring myself to smile. I was too conscious that its author was in pain."[14]

Between the Fraulein's appearances on the way to or in retreat from her daily battles with the Cockaloony Bird, the stage is held by two gossips, Polly and Molly. Molly is the landlady of the Big Dormitory, and she is ornery and penny-pinching. Polly is a gossip columnist who has come to spy on the decrepit Fraulein. The landlady and the gossip columnist delight in dwelling on the Fraulein's past and present misfortunes. Dressed in clown make-up and costumed in "pelican colors," they are the fiendish chorus to the Fraulein's frantic dance of death. But Williams punishes Polly. She is attracted to Indian Joe, "a blond Indian, tawny gold as a palamino horse but with Caribbean-blue eyes," who treats her with contempt. The low-minded gossip columnist is made to look ridiculous in panting for "an erotic fantasy" who rejects her. Joe, a peacock who humiliates all of the women in the play, is the objective embodiment of the Viennese dandy who insulted the Fraulein in front of international royalty.

With *The Gnadiges Fraulein,* Williams began to have his nightmares in public. This sad, overwrought play contains Williams's most frenzied presentation of the themes of loss of artistic power and the transience of fame that haunted him throughout the sixties.

After he had completed *Kingdom of Earth,* which was a return to a more controlled and traditional style of writing, Williams once again went to work on a play about a tortured artist. The painter in *In the Bar of a Tokyo Hotel* is no longer able to separate his life from his work. In *Out Cry,* Williams dramatizes his fears through an actor who is immobilized by childhood traumas and critical rejection. The Fraulein, the painter, and the actor are three harrowing self-portraits in which Williams approaches his writing as a form of therapy. The Gnadiges Fraulein has lost her beauty and renown—she is the artist as an old woman; the painter has lost himself in a new vision of the possibilities of art—he is the artist as madman and genius; the actor is haunted by memories of a withdrawn childhood—he is the artist as introverted child.

In both *Tokyo Hotel* and *Out Cry,* Williams deals with artistic crises in terms of a symbiotic male-female relationship: the artist and his wife, the actor and his sister, are totally dependent on each other. In both instances, the two characters are aspects of the same personality; the intense communion between male and female reflects the playwright's close identification with women. Before *Tokyo Hotel* opened, Williams said that the heroine of his new play is a "female monster, but I love her. I always love my women more than my men. I don't know why. Maybe it's the feminine in me."[15]

The play's driven artist is a weak man who needs his wife in order to survive. Mark is one of Williams's sacred aesthetes, a supremely sensitive artist in retreat from a brutish world. Exploring color, he has embarked on a mystical journey, creating a "new circle of light" where ordinary people cannot and dare not intrude. He is very fine—and very mad; and, as often in Williams, his madness is a sign of his special sensibility. The conflict between husband and wife—his aestheticism, her brashness—is thus a reversal of the antagonism in *Summer and Smoke,* in which the man is cast as the sexual pollutant to the woman's saint. Here, it is the woman who is earthy and coarse, the man who is otherworldly.

Mark may depend on Miriam and Williams may in fact "love" her, but few others are likely to react so favorably since the character is Williams's ultimate castrator. She is rapacious and acquisitive, and like Sebastian in *Suddenly Last Summer,* she goes through men like items on a menu. Wherever she goes, Miriam "absorbs" the atmosphere: "To absorb Kyoto wouldn't take me long. A woman of my vitality absorbs a place quickly. I could absorb a pagoda in a minute. . . . I look. I absorb. I go on." Barking orders in a gravelly, rum-soaked voice, she treats her husband as if he were her son, and she treats other men as if they were prostitutes available to the highest bidder.

The opening scene depicts her aggressive attack on the Japanese bartender. Wheedling, stroking, and grabbing, she punctuates her come-on with deep-throated laughter at her coarse jokes. She is more like a drag queen than a real woman.

Once [she reminisces] I was dancing with this attractive but inexperienced-looking young man—and I whispered in his ear: "Do you mind if I manipulate your genitals?"—Scared him out of. He said "Here?" as if he was in church. I said, "I'll step out for some air and you follow me out." Did he?—Hmmm.—You bet he did!—And I manipulated his genitals all right. —HMMM.—Yaisses!—Between a Cadillac and a—Hmmm—Cadillac.—Sure, we got into one.—Burrghh.—Recollections are insufficient. I like present action.

Martin Gottfried suggested that "her interest in men—like homosexuals'— runs to physical details (a concern with bodily hair and genital specifics) as does her humor ('Bangkok—what a name for a city!')."[16]

Miriam is a dragon lady, a witch, but Mark nevertheless depends on her strength. She is the manly comforter of his womanly fears; during his present crack-up, however, she decides she wants to leave, and she calls an art dealer friend of her husband's to come to Tokyo to arrange Mark's trip back to New York, and to confinement in a mental clinic.

During the two scenes in which he appears, Mark chants about his discovery of a circle of light. He is presented as a magician, a mystic, a mad saint. But his special insights do not save him. Mark's dedication to art is more fragile than Miriam's vitality, just as Blanche Du Bois's Old South gentility collapses when challenged by Kowalski's raw energy. Mark sees what average people cannot see, but he loses the ability to see the way normal people can and must see. Dazed by his work and feeling betrayed by his wife, he hangs himself.

Miriam survives precisely because she cannot enter her husband's "circle of light." Her "circle" has limits; "it is narrow. And protective. We have to stay inside. It's our existence and our protection. . . . It's our home if we have one. . . . This well-defined circle of light is our defense against. Outside of it there's dimness that increases to darkness: never my territory. It's never been at all attractive to me." For venturing beyond the protective and confining circle, Mark is heroic, and quite mad.

Rendered divine by his contact with art, Mark suffers for his aspirations beyond the normal human "circle." Although Miriam has the power to save her husband, she chooses to be a destroyer. She used to clip flowers outside Mark's studio. "When I heard you clipping flowers," Mark says, "it would sometimes occur to me that you wished the flowers you were clipping were [mine]." Together, for a while, they help each other to continue; alone, they are terrified. After Mark's suicide, Miriam says, "I have no plans. I have nowhere to go."

In the Bar of a Tokyo Hotel frustrated critics and audiences. More than ever before, reviewers accused Williams of using drama as private therapy.

I don't think anyone should be allowed to see it . . . a terribly naked work that reveals more about its author than he could have possibly intended.[17]

The play seems almost too personal, and as a result too painful, to be seen in the cold light of public scrutiny.[18]

. . . a play by a man at the end of, not his talent (that was long ago), but his tether. . . . That someone who was a major American and world dramatist should come to this is a tragedy almost unparalleled in the annals of literature, never mind drama.[19]

. . . so dreadfully self-pitying, in the most embarrassingly self-glorifying ways, that simply to describe it is to seem cruel.[20]

Life took out a full-page advertisement in *The New York Times:*

Played out? Tennessee Williams has suffered an infantile regression from which there seems no exit. . . . nothing about *In the Bar of a Tokyo Hotel* deserves its production. That's the kind of play it is, and that's the kind of play it gets in this week's *Life.* From a theatre review that predicts the demise of one of America's major playwrights to a newsbreaking story that unseats a Supreme Court judge, we call a bad play when we see it.[21]

The play didn't deserve the cruel pronouncements of doom it provoked; Williams was correct when he said that it "was not as bad as the critics said it was." But it is not a fully developed drama either. Miriam is a Williams stereotype, and Mark is more a collection of theories about art than a fully realized character. All too obviously, Mark speaks for the playwright's own feelings about his work: "An artist has to lay his life on the line"; "the images flash in my brain, and I have to get them nailed down on canvas at once"; "sometimes the interruption of work, especially in a new style, causes a, causes a—loss of momentum that's never recovered!"; "after the work, so little is left of me. To give to another person."

Concentrating on language more than on story or character development, Williams experiments with a lean, allusive, poetically charged diction. Monologues are held to a minimum, and the characters speak to each other in uncharacteristically brief, cryptic utterances. Although Williams depends, as usual, on repetition and the inversion of normal word order, the language is simpler than is standard for him. Many sentences end abruptly in mid air, such as Mark's comment, "no separation between myself and." Williams intends the device to signal the artist's inability to connect to the world around him, but since all the characters are often unable to complete their sentences, the technique seems merely affected.

Compared to *Out Cry,* however, *In the Bar of a Tokyo Hotel* is a well-made play. Williams feels particularly attached to *Out Cry* because it is his most deeply private play. The New York version produced in 1973 followed earlier renditions of the material presented in London and Chicago under the title *The Two-Character Play.*

In his other plays about tormented artists, Williams disguises himself as an ex-Follies star, a circus performer, and a painter, while in *Out Cry* the milieu is the theater and the two characters are a brother and sister who are the leading performers in a broken-down touring company. The two actors are as neurotic, and as dependent on each other, as the painter and his wife in *Tokyo Hotel.*

Felice and Clare are deserted by their company; "your sister and you are—insane," the telegram reads. Yet on a bare stage in an empty theater, the wretched pair rehearse compulsively for the show that must go on. They choose the only possible play in the repertory, *Two-Character Play,* which is a retelling of their own traumatic childhoods. The rehearsal therefore mixes past with present suffering; pivots illusion against reality; and merges life with theater. Their present imprisonment in the darkened theater echoes their reclusive childhood, when they were entombed in a dark house surrounded by sunflowers. Felice and Clare were the neighborhood freaks: "My brother Felice and I are surrounded by so much malice," Clare announces, "that we almost never, we hardly ever dare to go out of the house."

Their bohemian father shot their straitlaced mother and then killed himself, thereby voiding the children's inheritance. Cut off by this family scandal from the world beyond the encircling and protective sunflowers, the children are terrified of leaving their house, creating a private, fragile world for themselves. The greatest challenge is for them to walk without fear the one and one-half blocks to Grossman's Market. Most of the time they remain trapped in their house. "Magic is the habit of our existence," they claim; and so they turn to the unfinished autobiographical play as a refuge from their present confinement. Like the crazed artist in *Tokyo Hotel,* they are unable to separate their life from their art, and they become "lost in the play."

These two forlorn performers are familiar Williams types who ask for audience pity and understanding. Their fears of hostile audiences and their need to continue in the face of critical rejection reflect the playwright's own concerns. And their extreme closeness recalls Williams's deep attachment to his sister Rose. Williams, in fact, claims that the play "says everything" for him about his withdrawn childhood, about his intense feelings of being different because of his homosexuality.

As a statement by Williams on the nature and function of theater, and as a glimpse into his attitudes toward his work and his audience, *Out Cry* is of genuine interest. But considered apart from the troubled and celebrated personality who created it, the play fails utterly. It is deeply felt, but it is not dramatic. As if anticipating critical reaction, Williams has Clare say, "I wonder sometimes if it isn't a little too personal, too special, for most audiences. . . . old Gwendolyn Forbes said that *Two-Character Play* is a tour de force, it's more like an exercise in performance by two star performers than like a play, a real play." Gwendolyn Forbes, unfortunately, was correct, for this is not a *real* play. It is a work in progress, a shrill, disorganized public confession.

In the fifties Williams converted his psychological history into exciting theatrical fantasies, whereas in *Out Cry,* he merely parades his suffering. The play, as a result, is self-pitying, but also self-glorifying because it links madness to a kind of divinity. For these characters, being different, being crazy, is a mark of special distinction. Charles Marowitz wrote about the London version that "if anyone other than Tennessee Williams had written *Two-Character Play* . . . it would have been stood up and mercilessly mowed down."[22] But since Williams did write it, the play compels our attention if not our approval.

8

DINGY BARS,
FLEA-BAG HOTELS
TENTATIVE NEW DIRECTIONS

From the defrocked Reverend T. Lawrence Shannon in *The Night of the Iguana* to the expiring painter in *In the Bar of a Tokyo Hotel* and the traumatized actors in *Out Cry*, Williams's sixties plays are preoccupied with characters who have failed in their professions. The characters are creations from Williams's "lost decade." Three plays written during this period, though *(The Mutilated, Kingdom of Earth,* and *Small-Craft Warnings),* are not about failure. Differing in mood, structure, and quality, the three plays are linked by their female protagonists, all of whom frequent bars and live in rundown hotels. The women in these plays are victims and losers, women without men, yet they act as if they belong to the world's elect. Williams respects their courage. In all three plays, Williams captures the tawdry, soiled quality of life as it is lived on The Ritz Men Only side of the Camino Real, and his blowsy, beleaguered heroines are vivid variations on character types he created in the forties and fifties.

After the extreme reactions to *In the Bar of a Tokyo Hotel,* critics were especially kind to *Small-Craft Warnings* (1972), and this modest piece was even heralded as Williams's comeback after a decade of decline. But it is little different in quality from Williams's ill-received sixties efforts since its loose structure is as undramatic as that of *Tokyo Hotel* and its down-and-out characters are as stereotypical as any in the plays of this period. "The press is very anxious to call *Small-Craft Warnings* my comeback," Williams noted, "but I don't see it that way. I wish they could just take it in stride. I'm not trying to come back to Broadway;

I wouldn't even if they wanted me to. I'm just continuing to do what I've always done, and that is writing plays. I can't do anything else."[1] The play opened in New York on Easter Sunday, and Williams was certainly aware of the symbolic implications: "It's embarrassing taste to open then . . . somebody is bound to make a crack about the Resurrection. They'll say the Resurrection didn't come off."[2]

The playwright correctly assessed *Small-Craft Warnings* as "a little play. . . . I hope it is reviewed as what it is—something that corresponds to a short story."[3] In the tradition of American barroom plays like *The Time of Your Life, The Iceman Cometh,* and *No Place to be Somebody,* Williams's play offers a procession of talkative drinkers, losers, and eccentrics. Williams treats the characters gently, and this may well be his most generous play. It is also his least theatrical, being essentially a collection of character portraits. More than ever before, he dispenses with a conventional story line; his characters interact, but they are primarily self-absorbed, and the play is punctuated with soliloquies during which characters step to center stage in order to confide directly to the audience. (An earlier version was called *Confessional.*) The set speeches do not interrupt the action—they *are* the action. The soliloquies are not included to advance the story, or to clarify conflict, or even to explain character motivation, but simply for their own sake, for their beauty of language, their sentiment and feeling.

The central character, Leona, who describes herself as a "faggot's moll," is a beautician who moves in her trailer from town to town, setting up residence in a local bar and offering to work in a shop without pay until the proprietor can appraise her ability. Throughout much of the play, she reminisces about the "death-day" of her brother; complains about her current roommate, a stud named Bill; and is on the warpath against her friend Violet. When she's had too much to drink, Leona can be tough, but she is a sentimentalist at heart. She's proud of her homosexual violinist brother, a young man whose life she describes as "a work of art":

My brother . . . had pernicious anemia from the age of thirteen and any fool knows a disease, a condition, like that would make any boy too weak to go with a woman, but he was so full of love he had to give it to something like his music. And in my work, my profession as a beautician, I never seen skin or hair or eyes that could touch my brother's. His hair was a natural blond as soft as silk and his eyes were two pieces of heaven in a human face, and he played on the violin like he was making love to it. . . . I'm proud that I've had something beautiful to remember as long as I live in my lifetime.

The brother, the sensitive, suffering homosexual, the person too rare and too fine to endure in a harsh world, is of course a recurrent figure in Williams's plays. Leona's fondly remembered brother hovers like a patron saint over the bedraggled denizens of the bar; whenever Leona reminisces about him, the lights dim, and we hear a melancholy, lyrical violin.

Williams uses Leona's appreciation of her brother's beauty as an indication of her own worth. Shrill and bossy, she is nevertheless decent and she is able to say "'life!' to life, like a song to God, and when I die, I'll say 'death' like a song to God, too, because I've lived in my lifetime and not been afraid of—changes."

Williams is fond of her. "She is the first really whole woman I have ever created and my first wholly triumphant character. She is truly devoted to life, however lonely—whether it be with a stud like Bill or some young faggot she takes under her wing because he reminds her of her brother."[4] Leona is strong and independent, but she's always seeking new companions. When two homosexuals enter the bar, she befriends the younger one, regarding him as a possible replacement for Bill. As she boasts, she is not afraid of changes, and it is her spirit of adventure that Williams celebrates. When she leaves the bar at the end of the play, heading in her trailer to a new town and a new bar, she recalls Williams's Byron in *Camino Real,* "making voyages" from the tag-end of the Camino Real into the terra incognita beyond it.

Despite her mean tongue and her bullying manner, she is one of Williams's few optimistic characters, and her "life to life" is the standard against which the other characters are judged. The older homosexual, in particular, is her adversary. He has lost the ability to be surprised by life, and he counters Leona's "'life' to life!" with a blasé "Oh, well."

This boy I picked up tonight, the kid from the tall corn country, still has the capacity for being surprised by what he sees, hears and feels in the kingdom of earth. All the way up the canyon to my place, he kept saying, I can't believe it, I'm here, I've come to the Pacific, the world's greatest ocean!—as if nobody, Magellan or Balboa or even the Indians had ever seen it before him; yes, like he'd discovered this ocean, the largest on earth, and so now, because he's found it himself, it existed, now, for

the first time, never before. . . . And this excitement of his reminded me
of my having lost the ability to say: "My God!" instead of just: "Oh,
well."

The character has contempt for the gay life:

There's a coarseness, a deadening coarseness, in the experience of most
homosexuals. The experiences are quick, and hard, and brutal, and the
pattern of them is practically unchanging. Their act of love is like the
jabbing of a hypodermic needle to which they're addicted but which
is more and more empty of real interest and surprise. This lack of
variation and surprise in their—"love life"—spreads into other areas of
—"sensibility."

The young man he is with has none of his sourness. Because he places
no artificial restrictions on ways to express affection, he responded to the
touch of his companion's hand on his knee—it was "a human touch."
Sleeping one night under the stars with a boy and a girl, he enjoyed
the closeness of the two bodies, uninterested in separating male from
female. This boy from Iowa is the antidote to the embittered and
defensive older homosexual, and like Leona, the young man leaves the bar
in order to "make voyages." The older man—the homosexual as effete
and decadent predator—recalls Sebastian in *Suddenly Last Summer*.
The bisexual boy, who has sex without guilt, is Williams's spokesman for
a new gay consciousness that is more openly expressed in *Memoirs*.
    The play's alcoholic doctor is another enemy to life:

The holy mysteries of—birth and—death. . . . They're dark as the face of
God whose face is dark because it's the face of a black man. . . . I've
always figured that God is a black man with no light on his face. He moves
in the dark like a black man, a Negro miner in the pit of a lightless coal
mine.

When he is called to deliver a premature baby, he kills both the mother
and the infant and stuffs the foetus into a shoebox. Leona fiercely opposes
this shattered old man, but she was unable to prevent him from perform-
ing the delivery of the child.
    Leona, the bisexual young man, and Monk, the steady, sympathetic
bartender, are the play's positive characters. The others survive as well
as they can. Violet, a good-hearted tramp who lives over an amusement
arcade in a room without a bath or running water; Steve, a dim short-

order cook who is her current beau; and Bill, Leona's roommate, are a sad group, "tiny abandoned vessels,"[5]—small craft. Violet and Steve provide low comedy relief. They are both dumb, easy-going transients who spend their lives in dirty furnished rooms, grimy bars, and plastic burger palaces. Violet uses sex as an antidote to her untidy life; she makes a religion of the phallus. "She's got some form of religion in her hands," Leona says, when Violet touches Bill under the table; "she's worshipping her idea of God Almighty in her personal church."

The Mutilated is a more somber and mystical view of the kind of transient characters who cluster around the bar in *Small-Craft Warnings*. Trinket is "the mutilated" because she has had one breast removed, but her friend Celeste is also scarred. They are both down-on-their-luck dames of the Quarter in New Orleans. A chorus presides over the play, singing a song of hope for all the world's mutilated people:

> I think the strange, the crazed, the queer
> Will have their holiday this year
> And for a while, A little while,
> There will be pity for the wild.
> A miracle, A miracle!
> A sanctuary for the wild.

The imminent transforming miracle hovers over the play as Trinket and Celeste quarrel and reconcile, as Celeste roams the streets of the Quarter, as Trinket hides in shame in her shabby genteel hotel room and then picks up a gruff sailor in a bar.

The two women are hopelessly battered and without dignity, yet they try to face their desperation bravely. Shunned by her family (she is their public shame, since she is a petty thief and a jailbird), Celeste has only her friendship with Trinket to rely on. With her refined airs and her proudly-displayed cut-glass decanters, Trinket is the queen of the flea-bag Silver Dollar Hotel. She is one of those Williams characters with a secret— she is deeply ashamed of her mastectomy.

Celeste and Trinket are a complementary pair. Celeste is proud of her firm breasts while Trinket tries frantically to disguise her mutilation; Celeste is outgoing while Trinket hides guiltily in her room. On Christmas Eve, at the end of the play, after the reconciled friends have had their own communion with a glass of Tokay and vanilla cream wafers, Celeste has a vision of Our Lady.

There was an elderly sister at Sacred Heart Convent School that received invisible presence, and once she told me that if I was ever cut off and forgotten by the blood of my blood and was homeless alone in the world, I would receive the invisible presence of Our Lady in a room I was in. She said that I would smell roses. I smell roses. She said I would smell candles burning. . . .—I feel it, yes, I feel it, I know it! Our Lady's in the room with us. . . . You opened the door of your heart and Our Lady came in!

Miraculously, the pain in Trinket's breast disappears.

For once, Williams's women are saved by a power other than sex. But the play does contain a black-clad cowboy who watches over the characters. Like Chris Flanders in *The Milk Train Doesn't Stop Here Any More,* Jack in Black suggests sex, mortality, and deliverance. Though he is intensely sexual, his appearance in the play signals

> The tolling of a ghostly bell
> that Cries out farewell, to flesh farewell,
> Farewell to flesh, to flesh farewell!

Although Jack in Black "stacks the deck . . . loads the dice and tricks the wheel," he gives the ladies a reprieve from "the tolling of a ghostly bell." An ambiguous figure, the cowboy eases the women's burdens, grants them absolution, but remains untouchable; he is the earthly counterpart to the women's vision of Our Lady, a *deus ex machina* who superintends the play's final miracle.

Like *The Gnadiges Fraulein,* its companion piece in *Slapstick Tragedy, The Mutilated* is a fantasy. With its series of short scenes, its singing chorus, and its mystical denouement, the play is one of Williams's most experimental efforts. It has a desperate quality, however, that made audiences squirm, and its hysterical religiosity seems to emanate from the playwright himself as well as the overwrought characters.

The heroine of Williams's 1968 comedy, *Kingdom of Earth,*[6] has much in common with the bedraggled heroines of *The Mutilated* and *Small-Craft Warnings.* A one-time show girl who was billed as The Petite Personality Kid, Myrtle is one of the playwright's silly, good-natured victims. After her singing group, The Mobile Hot Shots, came to a sad end, Myrtle began to wait on tables at a hash house. Myrtle is a "fleshy" and "amiably loud-voiced" bleached blond who wears a pink turtleneck sweater and tight checkered pants, and who takes pills to keep down "the heat of her nature."

Myrtle herself is similar to characters from other sixties plays, but *Kingdom of Earth* does not resemble the other plays of the period in either its theme or its tone.[7] It is a droll, idiosyncratic, ornery comedy about the contest between half brothers, Lot and Chicken, for the ownership of a farm. Myrtle is the pawn tossed between them: she is Lot's new wife who ends up being Chicken's whore. The brothers represent two distinct types of Williams males. Chicken is swarthy and animallike while Lot is a sensitive mama's boy. They had the same father, but their mothers were very different. Lot's mother was refined and aloof while Chicken's mother was a tempestuous mulatto servant.

Dark-complected Chicken lives in the cavelike ground-floor kitchen, the only warm room in the house. Like Val Xavier in *Battle of Angels,* he has a guitar ("a real man-size instrument"). He plays with his knife, using it to carve dirty words and pictures on the dilapidated kitchen table; and he drowns cats—pussies—in the flooded cellar: "Consciously or not," Williams notes, Chicken frequently "drops one of his large, dusky hands over his crotch, which is emphasized, pushed out, by his hip boots."

Working the land, he lives by a philosophy of "hardness." "A man and his life both got to be equally hard," he explains to Myrtle. "Made out of the same hard thing. Man, rock. Life, rock. Otherwise one will break and the one that breaks won't be life. The one that breaks is the soft one and that's never life." Chicken sees life as a battle between the hard and the soft, the body and the spirit. A traveling preacher told him he ought to "haul down those spiritual gates on his lustful body." He tried self-denial for a time, and he lost, deciding he was created without "spiritual gates" and was not cut out for salvation. Williams's muscular hero chooses pleasure on earth:

There's nothing in the world, in this whole kingdom of earth, that can compare with one thing, and that one thing is what's able to happen between a man and a woman, just that thing, nothing more, is perfect. . . . Yes, you could come home to a house like a shack, in blazing heat, and look for water and find not a drop to drink, and look for food and find not a single crumb of it. But if on the bed you seen you a woman waiting, maybe not very young or good-looking even, and she looked up at you and said to you "Daddy, I want it," why, then I say you got a square deal out of life. . . . That's how I look at it, that's how I see it now, in this kingdom of earth.

Chicken's philosophy is vigorous and life-affirming. He is the positive character in the contest for the farm. He is the victor, as the strong characters in Williams always are, though he is much less manacing a character than Stanley Kowalski. Chicken is a free spirit who wants more than anything to own the land on which he works, and who subdues both his half-brother and his new sister-in-law in order to claim his kingdom.

Lot's domain is his mother's gilt-edged upstairs bedroom and her refined little parlor, separated from Chicken's crude kitchen by a dark, narrow, womblike hallway. Lot is dying of tuberculosis, and he has married Myrtle so that she rather than his dreaded half-brother will inherit the land. But Lot has miscalculated, because oversexed Myrtle cannot defend herself against Chicken. Upon his arrival at the farm, Lot retreats to his mother's upstairs bedroom, and he is soon lost in memories of the past. Like Violet and Sebastian in *Suddenly Last Summer,* Lot and his mother lived an elegant life—from which Lot's bestial father was pointedly excluded. Consisting of a brutish father, a genteel mother who tries to disguise her passionate nature, and a sissified son, the Ravenstocks are a classic Williams family. Uncharacteristically, though, Williams turns his aesthete into a foolish figure since Lot is a "frail, delicately— you might say exotically—pretty youth" who dresses in one of his mother's faded ball gowns. Lot is not a match for Chicken, and he soon withdraws from the contest. A deranged remnant of the doomed Old South, Lot represents the dregs of a once-proud tradition.

Tossed between the two archetypal Williams males in their lopsided battle for control of the land is poor, defenseless Myrtle, the last of The Mobile Hot Shots. Her hasty marriage to Lot is typical of the farcical quality of her life. Passing by a television studio, Myrtle was picked as a contestant on a local hillbilly version of "Queen for a Day." She recites her troubles so entertainingly that she wins the crown, and the favor of Lot, who was in the audience. Before they know it, they're married on the air, and Myrtle is thrust into a family battle she does not understand. She becomes the unwitting pawn between the half-brothers, carrying messages from Lot's upstairs retreat to Chicken's downstairs lair. With each descent, Chicken's hold on her is strengthened. As she works for Lot, trying to wheedle from Chicken the paper that deeds the land to him following Lot's death, she is drawn more and more to Chicken. Like Stanley Kowalski locked in battle with Blanche Du Bois, Chicken treats Myrtle with open scorn, but Myrtle doesn't have Blanche's strength, and she soon becomes Chicken's woman.

The characters' sexual identities are reflected in their responses to the oncoming flood. Lost in his reveries, Lot dies before the coming of the flood—he is beyond sex. Myrtle is terrified of water, and depends on Chicken to save her from the encroaching flood—she is both attracted to and frightened by the unleashed force that Chicken's sexuality promises. Chicken alone is unafraid of the challenge of the flood, welcoming it as a test of his hardness. The approach of the orgasmic flood waters coincides with his inheritance of the land.

Who shall inherit the South? The decadent aesthete or the virile natural man? Here, in a less ambivalent way than usual, Williams accords the victory to the powerful male, for only Chicken's hardness is equal to the land and the flood. The play celebrates orgasmic force rather than aristocratic refinement, and Williams for once sides clearly with the realist rather than the aesthete.

Kingdom of Earth is a richly symbolic, modern-day allegory about Williams's beloved, benighted South. It is a briskly charged comedy that provides a refreshing departure from the gloom-ridden sixties plays.

Williams has often announced that he is a compulsive writer who must begin each day with several hours of work. He worries over his material, constantly revising plays that have already been produced and published, and working on new material even in the face of continued critical and commercial defeat. Williams's two most recent plays (unpublished at this writing), *Vieux Carré* and *The Red Devil Battery Sign,* are further attempts, like *Small-Craft Warnings* and *Kingdom of Earth,* to recapture various moods of his major work of the forties and fifties. By-passing the claustrophobic self-scrutiny of Williams's experimental period, these plays signal a return to earlier modes while at the same time Williams introduces new themes in his work. *Vieux Carré* is an autobiographical memory play that recalls the pattern of *The Glass Menagerie,* while *The Red Devil Battery Sign* is an overheated melodrama that in structure and tone is similar to *Sweet Bird of Youth.* Both dramas have strong passages with moments of lyrical and theatrical power and both are ultimately unsatisfactory, reminders once again that Williams's inspiration is fitful. Both plays were harshly received. *Vieux Carré* was produced on Broadway in the spring of 1977 and closed within a week. In its first incarnation, *The Red Devil Battery Sign* opened and closed in Boston in the summer of 1975, was produced (successfully) in a revised version, in Vienna (in English) in 1976, and then (unsuccessfully) in London in the summer of 1977.

The two plays, in attempting to transcend the thematic and stylistic despondency of works like *In the Bar of a Tokyo Hotel* and *Out Cry,* contain enough strong writing to testify to the fact that Williams's Southern myths still have theatrical validity. In sensibility and control, the voice is diminished—but it is not moribund.

Vieux Carré is a recycling, in a muted, autumnal mood, of characters and atmosphere Williams himself has made banal through overuse. It is set in a rundown New Orleans boarding house inhabited by a representative assortment of Williams's doomed outcasts: a consumptive painter, a tremulous fashion designer dying of leukemia, a callous barker for a strip joint, a photographer who throws orgiastic parties, two wildly eccentric elderly ladies, a tyrannical landlady, and a struggling young writer. The play is based on the author's reminiscences of his own experiences in just such an establishment. For the first time since *The Glass Menagerie,* Williams uses a narrator—himself, as a young man of twenty-eight, in love with writing and tentatively exploring his homosexuality. In a recent interview, Williams maintained that "the boy's personality is totally different from mine. He talks quite differently from the way that I talk, and yet the events in the house did actually take place.... Also, I did not leave there with a wealthy old sponsor (as the Young Man does)."[8] Far less emotional than the playwright himself, the Writer is in fact a wan master of ceremonies. Williams has observed him with affection, but as a dramatic character he is faint. Being kind to this image of his younger self, Williams has made him sweet-natured and sensitive while choosing to erase from the portrait the lusty, sardonic humor, the compulsive sexual hunger, the high-strung infatuation with art, of the young Williams in New Orleans as he appears in *Memoirs.* The Writer's speeches set the mood (he begins and ends the play with the elegy, "The house is empty now") without really clarifying his response to his environment or revealing his character to us.

Remaining a detached observer, he oversees the action without fully participating in it. Williams's mellow treatment of the play's host is symptomatic: this is a play of reminiscence which, quite unlike *The Glass Menagerie,* lacks dramatic conflict. Williams does not establish the importance to the Writer of his memories from the old rooming house, and we are never convinced that these sad, lost characters have affected him deeply as either an artist or a man.

Williams has assembled the materials for the play from a short story, "The Angel in the Alcove," and from a short play, "The Lady of Larkspur Lotion." The resulting mosaic construction has the feel of two uneasily linked one-act dramas. *Vieux Carré* consists basically of two confrontations between tenants: the first act is dominated by the Writer's meetings with the consumptive painter who lives in the adjoining cubicle; the second act is taken over by a prolonged argument between a pale Northern beauty and a husky Bourbon Street barker who lives with her. Presiding over the house, and along with the Writer-narrator, providing a loose continuity for the action, is Mrs. Wire, the landlady, a sour, penny-pinching woman who has little appreciation of the colorful, indigent, often deceitful people of the Quarter who hover under her roof. Mrs. Wire is a petty tyrant, capable of cruelties to her forlorn tenants, but she is not altogether heartless—there are remnants of gentleness in her manner. This is the third time Williams has written about Mrs. Wire (she is a principal figure in both "The Angel in the Alcove" and "The Lady of Larkspur Lotion"), and yet she remains a tiresome character superficially observed; we never learn more about her than her eccentricities, such as sleeping on a moldy cot in the hall to superintend the comings and goings of her sometimes raffish tenants. She remains simply a "character," one of the odd creatures that decorate Williams's world, though usually in peripheral roles. Like the Writer, Mrs. Wire is not a vigorous enough figure to support the central position she has been forced to occupy.

The painter who dominates the first act, however, is movingly drawn. Yet another of Williams's burnt-out cases, he is a truly dispossessed figure. What is new in the characterization is that Williams has made him a homosexual, and the character's seduction of the recalcitrant narrator is the first time in the plays that Williams has presented homosexuality—a subject he still does not want to devote a full-length play to—so openly. Unlike *Memoirs*, where gay life is often described as joyously sensual, the play evokes the dark side of the homosexual world: a life of compulsive cruising, fragmented relationships or totally anonymous sexual encounters. Saturated in the poetry of Hart Crane, Verlaine, and Rimbaud, the painter is well-acquainted with "the sound of loneliness" as he swallows his "sandman specials" to spare himself the anxieties of the night. Williams specifically equates the character's aching loneliness with his being a homosexual. The dying painter, coughing up blood, treated with contempt by Mrs. Wire, makes a desperate play for the innocent and evasive young man. At first dismissive, the Writer yields, offering himself to the older man the way other handsome young men in Williams's plays have soothed lonely women. For the first time in the plays, Williams's mystical connection between sex and religious salvation is seen in specifically homosexual terms.

The painter is the most memorable character in the play. And Williams's treatment of him proves that he can write of homosexual alienation and desire without being mawkish or sensational. The tone of the encounters between the Writer and the older man is carefully balanced; their scenes are written with a compassion that skirts outright sentimentality, and are charged with an earthy poetry.

The religious aura that encloses the older man's seduction of the narrator is embellished by the intermittent appearance, throughout the play, of an angel in the alcove: a vision of the Writer's Grandmother, who represents an image of security. The "angel" visits him in moments of crisis or despair; and when he no longer sees her, he decides it is time to leave Mrs. Wire's house. Williams's use of religious motifs, here as in *The Mutilated,* is wildly sentimental, but it indicates an abiding faith in the symbols of Christianity which he testifies to in *Memoirs.*

The second act offers a more traditional Williams encounter. A refined woman has taken in an irresponsible man, and now she wants to end their relationship. Dying of leukemia, she has thought of the muscular young man as her salvation. Here once again Williams opposes a puritan against a cavalier, the woman drawn irresistibly to her lover's sexual power, and repelled by her need for him. Though she knows the man is not worthy of her, she is blocked in her efforts to expel him by her fear of being alone and by the strength of her desire. Written according to the familiar Williams patterns, and missing the poetry and tenderness of the explicitly homosexual episode in the first act, the long scene between these pale echoes of Blanche and Stanley is stale, the characters' impact undermined by Williams's overuse of their types. Nevertheless, their brawl, enacted on a broiling summer afternoon and punctuated by the voices of cackling tourists being shown the garden and facade of this once-grand house in the French Quarter, has a pungent atmosphere. Williams works up a sense of the characters' confinement, and their entrapment within their room as well as their entrapment of each other is forcefully conveyed.

An uneasy mixture of old and new patterns, *Vieux Carré* is a minor mood piece that deserves more of a hearing than it received. Williams has said that he thought at first "it was a big mistake to transfer a story of mood ["The Angel in the Alcove"] to the stage."[9] His concern that the material would seem "insubstantial," however, was justified, for *Vieux Carré* seems like evocative short stories transferred to an alien medium.

Written before *Vieux Carré*, *The Red Devil Battery Sign* partakes of none of the sexual disclosures nor the confessional aura of parts of the later play and all of *Memoirs* and *Moise and the World of Reason*. And yet, as in *Vieux Carré*, Williams introduces a new element into his dramaturgy, this time the novel theme being contemporary politics. Williams offered a political background in *Sweet Bird of Youth*, though purely for local color; in *The Red Devil Battery Sign*, he uses a political setting in a way that is more central to his theme, with predictably mixed results. The play is set in Dallas, shortly after the Kennedy assassination, and Williams borrows from that event a pervasive atmosphere of menace. The heroine (called Woman Downtown—Williams favors nameless characters in these late plays) is married to a big business mogul, head of a right-wing cartel called the Red Devil Battery; he and his associates, or so the woman claims, are planning a take-over of the government. The woman is being kept a prisoner in the Yellow Rose Hotel because apparently, her husband suspects that she plans to expose him to a congressional committee. The woman eventually tries to escape from the hotel, is captured by her husband's henchmen, who in turn are attacked by a roving anarchist gang. After she is raped by the gang, the heroine decides to join forces with them—like many Williams heroines before her, she equates sexual violation with a kind of salvation and renewal. At the end she tosses bombs at some of the big buildings owned by the omnipresent Red Devil empire.

The plotting is delirious, and as a political statement, the play is both untenable and confused: is Williams supporting indiscriminate bomb throwing as the proper means to resist a right-wing dictatorship? Have rape and political radicalization freed Woman Downtown of the demons that have haunted her throughout the play? The play's choices—between a right-wing take-over and total anarchy—are nightmarish distortions of political realities. Williams sexualizes politics, the anarchist gang charged with a potent sexuality, the right-wing empire a group of faceless men in business suits. The play ends with a powerful apocalyptic image as Woman

Downtown and the band of modern werewolves howl madly in a fog-bound swamp on the edge of the city. In its suggestions of cosmic doom, the play has echoes of *Suddenly Last Summer.*

Williams of course is neither a political thinker nor a social dramatist. Williams said about the play that its theme is "the moral decay of our country in 1963—and our disengagement.... None of my plays is political, yet all of them are social documents—reflecting social conditions."[10] This first attempt of his at a political statement about America is naively drawn and extremely generalized, the lack of specific details designed to promote an aura of menace, as in Pinter, but also perhaps to disguise Williams's own shallow knowledge of politics. Williams is sympathetic to liberal causes—he has even claimed at times to be a Socialist—but his deepest responses are to sexuality rather than politics, and not surprisingly, the play treats the political threat of an omnivorous military-industrial complex as a symbolic field against which the distraught heroine enacts her paranoia and sense of entrapment. Political take-over haunts the heroine's imagination the way Blanche and Amanda are bewitched by memories of the gracious antebellum South: politics, that is, becomes a new symptom of the neurosis of a Williams character. Whether or not the Woman Downtown is only creating the concept of the overthrow as part of her generally hysterical condition is left, deliberately, unclear.

With its B movie use of mysterious documents, hooded ruffians, and its overexcited vocabulary of conspiracy, the play is more dependent on incident and on storyline than any drama Williams has written except for his Gothic thriller, *Suddenly Last Summer.* The plot details shade into the abstractions and generalizations of allegory, but, as a story, a political thriller with a genuinely ominous denouement, *The Red Devil Battery Sign* is engrossing. The play falters, as is the case with *Vieux Carré,* not when Williams is investigating some fresh elements in his writing, but when he relies on patterns of conflict that have long since become merely conventional in his work. Perhaps uncertain of the political details of his story, Williams becomes sidetracked by an elaborately developed relationship between the Woman Downtown and King, a typical middle-aged he-man (reminiscent of Angelo Mangiacavallo in *The Rose Tattoo*) who is suffering from brain damage as a result of a car accident. (Leukemia, consumption, brain damage: Williams is these latest plays persists in subjecting his characters to ghastly medical histories, no doubt symptomatic of his own nagging foreboding of imminent doom.) King was formerly the leader of a mariachi band, and he comes to the hotel where the heroine is imprisoned in order to visit his musicians and to reminisce about his former eminence. Williams becomes absorbed by the doomed romance between a vigorous man losing his vitality and a ravenous, alcoholic woman. There are long scenes between the two characters in which Williams expands on their psychological histories, the woman recalling a traumatic childhood in a rich family where her current fears of confinement were clearly germinated, and a series of incarcerations in asylums, the man detailing his incestuous attachment to his daughter, a flamenco dancer, and his devotion to his possessive wife. The man's domestic life is enacted in lengthy and thematically pointless scenes of familial squabbling.

Williams was clearly taken with King, and the part is expanded far beyond what is necessary to the political fable. The character is a blend of the vitality and the sense of defeat that mark Williams's own psychological swings. King's failing powers, his diminished control over both his art and his mind, reflect once again Williams's own sense of loss. Williams gives the character a florid death scene in which King, facing blindness and imminent insanity as a result of his brain tumor, commits suicide.

There is much here that is shrill, giddy, merely preposterous, as there are also great intensity and moments of rhetorical power. Williams hasn't mastered the material yet—it is almost as if there are two plays here, the foreground romantic drama imperfectly assimilated to the sketchy but enticing allegory of fascism and anarchy. At the moment, *The Red Devil Battery Sign* is a play in the making, a concept with the potential of becoming a chilling vision of contemporary apocalypse. Untidy as it is, though, the play has size and daring and a fevered theatrical imagination; it is a testament to Williams's enduring, embattled creative powers.[11]

9

FILM ADAPTATIONS

With their lush and literary imagery, their cascading set speeches, their absorption with character at the expense of traditional narrative interest, their concentrated time spans, limited settings, and confined action, the plays of Tennessee Williams are deeply theatrical. And yet these proscenium-bound concepts have been translated into successful and stylistically influential films that challenge rigid preconceptions about what is theatrical and what is cinematic. The films based on Williams's plays retain the spirit of the originals, so that even when Williams did not work on the screenplays, his personality and vision dominate. Appropriately, the films are always advertised with the playwright's name above the title; and even as his Broadway reputation dimmed in the sixties, Williams continued to be marquee bait at the movies.

From *The Glass Menagerie* in the late forties to *Boom* and *The Last of the Mobile Hot Shots* in the late sixties, Hollywood studios have been drawn to Williams's material. Because of his belief in the power of youth and glamor and money, because he is obsessively concerned with sex, because he uses exotic settings and delights in decadence and deviation, Williams fills many of the requirements for popularly conceived movies. Like the good box-office melodramatist he is, Williams thrives on explosive sexual conflicts. Though it is both private and defiantly individual, Williams's world is yet instantly recognizable to mass audiences— Williams is eccentric yet accessible, and until his most recent work this quality has been one of the sources of his great popular appeal. Williams's dramas have emotional rather than intellectual complexity; they are wise about universal needs and fears, and it is exactly this kind of material, with its immediate sensory impact, that popularly oriented films can make use of.

Throughout the fifties, Williams's name signaled mature themes—the playwright "educated" Hollywood as he had Broadway. Most of his plays of the forties and fifties deal with sexual maladjustments and obsessions that were daring in their day: Williams's men were sexier than the Hollywood norm, his women more frustrated and passionate. Williams's fifties movies were popular because they were audacious and novel. Sometimes, filmmakers regarded the original material as too unsavory for general audiences. On stage, Chance Wayne in *Sweet Bird of Youth* is punished in a typical Williams manner—he fails to get the girl and he is castrated. But the movie version gives him the girl and the town bullies only punch him up a little. *A Streetcar Named Desire* also made its producers nervous since they weren't confident that audiences would accept Stella's return to Stanley; and the film concludes with the brutalizing hero deserted (at least temporarily) by his enraged wife.

In their own shifty way, *Cat on a Hot Tin Roof* and *Suddenly Last Summer* were early movie treatments of homosexuality. Richard Brooks's film of *Cat* tries strenuously to avoid the then-taboo subject; Brooks claimed that Brick's problem wasn't homosexuality at all but simply his reluctance to transcend a star athlete's high school mentality. Despite the masquerade, however, Brick's exceptional feeling for his friend Skipper is present in the film, and seems to explain his reluctance to sleep with his wife.

With Gore Vidal's assistance, Joseph L. Mankiewicz tried to gloss over Sebastian's perverse tastes, but *Suddenly Last Summer* still emerges as the homosexual nightmare fantasy it is: an imperious gay poet is eaten alive by the boys he has courted and abandoned. The movie hinted at a subject and a milieu—homosexual cruising patterns—neither familiar to nor tolerated by the general moviegoing public.

Williams's major run-in with prevailing movie morality, however, was with *Baby Doll.* Carroll Baker sucking her thumb while lying scantily clad in a crib was considered an assault on the sensibility of mid-fifties America. From the pulpit of St. Patrick's Cathedral in New York, Cardinal Spellman denounced the film as "salacious," "blatant," "prurient." Williams was amazed, as indeed he ought to have been, for *Baby Doll* is one of his most benign works, and certainly much less troublesome in its treatment of sex than any of the other fifties films.

The question of morality aside, *Baby Doll* occupies a special place in the Williams canon since it is his only original screenplay (it is based on two one-act plays). With its lively characters, its atmospheric Southern setting, its witty, pungent dialogue, and its teasing sex, *Baby Doll* is a forceful demonstration of the suitability of Williams's work to films. *Baby Doll* is a gutsy, playful heterosexual comedy (for a change, there are no masked homosexual relationships here, and nobody could accuse Baby Doll of being a man in drag). The film, which is about Baby Doll's seduction by a fiery Sicilian, is as blithely amoral as its sleazy, low comedy, Southern white trash characters. In a sporting mood, Williams experiments with variations on his Southern Gothic repertory, placing at the center of his story a nubile, desirable woman rather than his usual male model. Baby Doll is dumb, common, and sexy, and Archie Lee, her fat, middle-aged husband, nearly goes wild with desire for her. But Baby Doll is a Lolita-like tease who perversely refuses to allow her husband in her bed.

The screenplay therefore presents a comic reversal of the thwarted marriage in *Cat on a Hot Tin Roof,* with Archie Lee panting, like Maggie the Cat, for the withheld pleasures of a spouse's body. Williams appreciates Maggie, and he regards Brick with the awe he usually reserves for his handsome and reluctant studs. But for the gross Archie Lee and the foolish Baby Doll he has only scorn.

A child-woman who entered into marriage with the proviso that she wouldn't perform her wifely duties until her twentieth birthday, Baby Doll is a case of arrested development. Sleeping in a crib, sucking her thumb, strolling distractedly through the house in abbreviated costumes, Baby Doll is a droll black comedy version of Brick. Brick's block against sex is serious, though, and Williams considers it seriously, if evasively; but Baby Doll's refusal to sleep with her husband is merely the whim of a spoiled little girl.

This stalled marriage, with Archie Lee spying on his wife through holes in the plaster and Baby Doll alternately taunting and rebuffing her feverish husband, is sparked by the intrusion of Silvio Vaccaro, one of Williams's lusty foreign characters. Archie Lee has burnt down Vaccaro's cotton mill because Vaccaro is his successful competitor; and Vaccaro comes sniffing around Archie Lee's house in order to collect evidence against him. The encounter between Vaccaro and Baby Doll is the center of the film. As Vaccaro plies Baby Doll for information, scoring on her attraction to him, and cunningly proffering and then withdrawing his interest in her, he conducts a languorous, richly comic seduction. Poor Baby Doll, like most Williams women, is a goner, for she is a hot-blooded girl who has kept unnatural restraints on her physical urges—and this dark, sultry stranger exudes all the passion so conspicuously missing in her husband. At first, playing the game she is used to working with Archie Lee, she is coy, secure in the power of her charms. But she is unused to such a sly opponent. Vaccaro knows precisely when to cool his ardor, and when he simmers down, her interest is aroused. Expertly, he manipulates his victim's fear of and attraction to sex. The heavy-breathing scene on the swing (in 1956 it was this more than anything else that made the censors edgy); the cat-and-mouse chase through the decaying house, Vaccaro at one point straddling a rocking horse with lascivious delight; and the showdown in the crumbling attic are the chief "stations" of Vaccaro's virtuoso seduction.

Williams is playing a pretty sly game himself, because at the end we don't know for sure if Baby Doll's virginity is still intact. Archie Lee thinks he has lost her, and his suspicions drive him to a gun-crazed revenge (he is carted away, screaming like a maniac). But what about Baby Doll? Is she untouched? Are she and her dotty Aunt Rose Comfort to move in with Vaccaro? Or are they to rot away, uncared for, in the ramshackle mansion? Did Williams have his eye on the censor, or is the ambiguity simply part of the film's playful spirit?

With *Baby Doll* Williams is in a relaxed mood. This droll, naughty story is a pleasing interlude between the experiments of the early fifties *(The Rose Tattoo, Camino Real)* and the three dark plays *(Orpheus Descending, Suddenly Last Summer, Sweet Bird of Youth)* of the late fifties. Williams laces his low comedy variations on his familiar types with a suggestion of a plot and a wonderfully seedy backdrop—a decaying mansion, its rooms ludicrously bare or inappropriately furnished, with baby cribs, for instance; its walls peeling and cracking, its floors and ceilings noticeably giving way. Ornery, downbeat, marching to the beat of its own rhythm, *Baby Doll* is acted with Method intensity and swagger by Carroll Baker, Karl Malden, Eli Wallach, and Mildren Dunnock and directed by Elia Kazan with full appreciation of Williams's sardonic comedy.

Because Williams's settings are always exotic, and drenched in Southern atmosphere, the film versions of the plays are all visually interesting. It doesn't matter whether or not the films open up the proscenium-created material. The movie of *Streetcar,* for instance, is confined for the most part to the Kowalski's dingy apartment, and yet the film is not static. With its ominous shadows, prominent spotlights, tight close-ups, and sharp camera angles, the film has a rich, brooding texture, a compelling visual personality. Many of the films, and especially *Baby Doll, The Rose Tattoo,* and *The Fugitive Kind,* have the same sweaty, steamy Southern Gothic ambience. Dilapidated mansions and crumbling one-horse towns are rendered in grainy black and white. The films give the settings independent life.

The plays don't need much rearranging or restructuring in order to work successfully as films; and those adaptations that stay the closest to Williams's original concepts are usually the most effective. *Cat on a Hot Tin Roof,* except for some brief opening shots, sensibly restricts itself to the Pollitt estate, switching the action only from the bedroom to the living room to Big Daddy's cellar with its remnants of his European travels. *The Last of the Mobile Hot Shots* (the film title for *Kingdom of Earth*) moves back and forth between the play's two symbolic settings, the faded upstairs bedroom and the primitive downstairs kitchen. The two rooms reflect the characters of their occupants; except for a brisk opening sequence, which depicts Lot's hasty marriage to Myrtle and their honeymoon trip through funny-looking small towns and a rain-soaked countryside, the movie is confined to the symbolically-charged rooms.

Williams's limited settings, then, are rich in visual possibilities for an imaginative director. Joseph Losey's underrated movie version of *The Milk Train Doesn't Stop Here Any More* (called *Boom*) looks stunning. The story is enacted against one of Williams's lushest settings, a pink villa overlooking the Mediterranean, and Losey gives the film a schematic color design consisting of bright whites and pinks and blues, and he furnishes Flora Goforth's mansion in an aptly flamboyant style. Losey brings Flora's house to life in a way that a stage production never could; the house seems to take on a personality of its own.

None of the films drastically refashions Williams's original ideas, but the most adventurously structured films, for the most part, fare least well. *Sweet Bird of Youth* is a sloppy play. For once, Williams was hampered by the physical confinements of the proscenium, and he had difficulty not only in getting all of his characters into the hotel in which the action is set but also in conveying their intersecting personal histories. As it resorts to clumsily-inserted flashbacks to account for the characters' past, the film becomes a structural shambles. Its fractured narrative method overcomes Williams's talky exposition, but it also weakens the drama: on stage, *Sweet Bird* has speed and intensity despite its lopsided construction; on film, the abrupt transitions between past and present, the multiple settings—all the conventional devices, in short, that movies use to open up stage properties—cut into the drive, the manic build-up, of the original.

Period of Adjustment also suffers from a fear of claustrophobia. Williams ends the play with a theatrical device: the two squabbling couples reconcile simultaneously as the spotlight shifts from bedroom to living room. Like the play itself, this ending is banal, but what power it does have comes from concentration. To avoid the stigma of filmed theater, the movie places the couples in so many different locations that Williams's verbal texture is dissipated. *Period of Adjustment* looks like a play half-heartedly expanded for the movies. Not surprisingly, Williams's most superficially conventional drama, a stab at Broadway domestic comedy, is the least flavorful Williams film—MGM gloss with moments of good acting and dialogue.

But the film that most expands on a Williams original—*Suddenly Last Summer*—is also, paradoxically, the best Williams film (though the playwright himself does not think so). Flamboyantly visual, the film moves away from the play's symbolic, hothouse jungle garden and takes us inside the local mental asylum. The film dramatizes the events described in the heroine's long concluding monologue about what happened last summer under the blazing white sun of Cabeza de Lobo. The final sequence, depicting the events leading up to Sebastian's martyrdom, is a tour de force of direction in which images complement Catherine's monologue to splendid effect. The play's final, pulsing set speech lends itself to visualization in a way that most Williams mood-memory monologues do not; Catherine's confession is enhanced by the film's staccato rhythms and strikingly composed images.

Williams influenced the style of all his collaborators; but two in particular, scene designer Jo Mielziner and Elia Kazan, are especially indebted to him. Working to the demands of Williams's idiosyncratic material, Mielziner and Kazan evolved the trademarks of their own styles. A Mielziner set, with its wispy, fanciful mixture of realism and expressionism, its blend of objective and subjective detail, its tilts and angles, is a distinctive artifact that has influenced stage design since the late forties. Kazan did not fully develop his style until he worked with Williams on *Streetcar*. It is likely that some of Kazan's most famous films, including *East of Eden* and *A Face in the Crowd,* were directly inspired in their mood and pacing and handling of actors, by Kazan's exposure to Williams's Southern Gothic dramas.

Kazan is pre-eminently an actor's director who brought to American films a new level of naturalistic performance. Method-drenched, both casual and intense, with its battery of the pause, the stammer, the back-track, and the overlap, the Kazan-directed performance presented the actor in new guises—as neurotic, as slob, as inarticulate rebel. Yet Williams was the catalyst whose fantasies inspired the genius of both Kazan and of Brando. Without Williams's Kowalski, Brando's career would not have been launched as spectacularly as it was—and Brando's playing of Williams's character revolutionized American film acting.

Williams is our foremost actor's playwright, comparable to Chekhov in his generosity to performers. The Actors Studio developed virtually as an adjunct to Williams's work the way Stanislavski's theories of acting evolved in relation to Chekhov's plays. Like Chekhov, Williams demands a heightened kind of realistic acting and the willingness of actors to explore their own neurotic conflicts. The performance of Williams's dramas startled New York in the forties and early fifties the way the Moscow Art Theater's rendering of Chekhov had surprised turn-of-the-century Russia.

Like the famous Broadway productions, the Williams films are a legacy of virtuoso acting: Brando, coiled, rapt, explosive, and Vivien Leigh, suffering transcendently, in *Streetcar;* Anna Magnani as the explosive Serafina in *The Rose Tattoo;* Carroll Baker as the delightfully perverse Baby Doll; Paul Newman as the cool, troubled stud in *Cat on a Hot Tin Roof* and *Sweet Bird of Youth;* Geraldine Page as the fluttering, distraught Alma Winemiller in *Summer and Smoke;* Burl Ives, indelible as Big Daddy; Warren Beatty as the arrogant hustler in *The Roman Spring of Mrs. Stone;* Elizabeth Taylor and Katharine Hepburn as the high-strung adversaries in *Suddenly Last Summer.*

Since they are usually playing volatile, overwrought characters, actors in a Williams role are expected to make spectacles of themselves. Drawing on the tricks of the Method, summoning sense impressions and burrowing into their own memories to find "emotional equivalents" for their charac-ters, the actors, like the playwright himself, are prey to self-parody. The same manner used too often inevitably yields diminishing results. Geraldine Page made her reputation as spinsterlike Alma Winemiller, but the actress has used the technique evolved for Alma over and over again; and the high-pitched, breathy voice, the peculiar phrasing, the hands to hair gesture that worked so well, that seemed so fresh, for Alma, have paled in the service of weaker roles. She has used her Williams-inspired manner too many times now in order to embellish threadbare material.

Adult, distinctive, visually interesting, acted and directed with energy and occasional inspiration, the films based on Tennessee Williams's plays provide some of Hollywood's proudest moments. Faithful to the playwright's original material, the films have been designed to preserve the twists and kinks, the spectacular and fabled neuroses, of our national poet of the perverse.

10

SOME CONCLUDING NOTES

Recently, Tennessee Williams has said that in the last decade he abandoned the realistic mode that sustained him through the early part of his career. But he has never been a traditional realist, for his plays have always been heightened, theatrical, sometimes gaudy fantasies derived from his own neuroses.

Williams is not a skillful storyteller. His narrative abilities are meagre, and in the work of the last dozen years, burrowing deeper and deeper into his own problems, he has practically eliminated plots from his dramas.

Williams, as he often says himself, is not an intellectual writer. By means of his symbols, he tries to give his work thematic weight, but we do not read him for the depth or originality of his ideas. The playwright with whom he has least in common is George Bernard Shaw.

We do not read Williams for the clarity of his statements either, for he is often a muddled thinker and an addled psychologist. Because he has mixed feelings about many of his characters, he often has difficulty in finding a suitable destiny for them.

Williams is not a social dramatist. Social movements, politics, "causes" —these have no part in the Williams play. His work cannot be read as any sort of social index of mid-century America, except insofar as the sexuality of his characters—and Williams's treatment of their sexuality— can be said to reflect the times.

We do not read Williams, then, for his ideas, or for his stories, or for his depiction of contemporary affairs. We read him instead for the surging emotion of the plays, for his tortured, contradictory, often sexually masked, passionate characters and the resounding conflicts in which they are entrapped, and for his pulsating, intense language. Williams's speciality is the long monologue in which a disturbed character recollects a dramatic moment. In these passages, as indeed throughout most of his work, Williams's writing is a blend of florid imagery, incantatory repetition, and labyrinthine syntax.

Williams is often confused about how he feels for his muscular men and desperate women, but his haunted, dispossessed, mutilated characters are among the most vivid in American drama. Williams's symbolism may sometimes be strained, his thematic aspirations may be pretentious, but his colorful, neurotic characters are joyously theatrical: Williams has created more great parts for actors than any other modern playwright.

As a young man, Williams recognized that the name Tennessee Williams had a more commercial appeal than the plain "Tom Williams" with which he was born. Williams has never lost his sense of showmanship, and even in his period of decline, he has continued to try to stimulate and surprise audiences, to give them a good show that also has some important things to say about love, sex, loneliness, and art.

Williams has always been a private and inward-looking writer, but in the late forties and fifties, his personal fantasies were transformed into dramas that had immense popular appeal. Williams lost much of his audience in the sixties, and he hasn't written a commercially or critically successful play since *The Night of the Iguana* in 1961. In the long view, however, his position as one of America's most forceful and original playwrights is assured.

NOTES

1. THE MAN AND HIS WORK

1. "Interview with Tennessee Williams," *Playboy* (April 1973), p. 69.
2. Tom Driver, *The New Republic* (April 20, 1959), p. 21.
3. Funke and Booth, "Williams on Williams," *Theatre Arts* (January 1962), p. 18.
4. Arthur Gelb, "Williams and Kazan and the Big Walk-Out," *New York Times* (May 1, 1960).
5. Quoted in *Time* (April 11, 1960), p. 77.
6. Don Ross, *New York Herald Tribune* (March 3, 1957).
7. Tennessee Williams, "Survival Notes," *Esquire* (September 1972), p. 168.
8. Rex Reed, "Tennessee Williams Turns Sixty," *Esquire* (January 1972), p. 108.
9. Mike Wallace, *New York Post* (December 30, 1957).
10. *New York Times* (March 8, 1959).
11. *New York Herald Tribune* (March 8, 1959).
12. John Weisman, *Tropic* (February 20, 1972), p. 30.
13. Edwina Dakin Williams, *Remember Me to Tom*, p. 34.
14. Clive Hirschhorn, *Sunday Express* (London) (March 28, 1965).
15. Margaret Laing, *The Sunday Times* (London) (March 28, 1965).
16. *Playboy*, p. 72.
17. *Time* (March 9, 1962).
18. Marion Magid, "The Innocence of Tennessee Williams," p. 43.
19. *Playboy*, p. 74.
20. *Saturday Review* (April 29, 1972), p. 29.
21. Nancy Tischler, *Tennessee Williams: Rebellious Puritan*, p. 295.
22. *Time* (March 9, 1962), p. 60.
23. Tennessee Williams, introduction to *Reflections in a Golden Eye* by Carson McCullers (Norfolk: New Directions, 1950), p. xii.

24. Richard Gray, *The Literature of Memory. Modern Writers of the American South* (Baltimore: The Johns Hopkins University Press, 1977), p. 258.
25. Magid, p. 34.

2. THE BATTLE OF ANGELS

1. *Boston Globe* (December 31, 1940).
2. *Variety* (January 1, 1941).
3. Marjory Adams, *Boston Globe* (September 17, 1945).
4. Ibid.
5. *Boston Post* (January 19, 1941).
6. Richard Hayes, *Commonweal* (April 26, 1957), pp. 956–57.
7. *Boston Herald* (September 20, 1945).
8. Ibid.
9. *Boston Herald* (October 6, 1945).
10. Joseph Wood Krutch, *The Nation* (October 6, 1945), p. 349.
11. *Boston Herald* (October 6, 1945).
12. Euphemia van Rensselaer Wyatt, *Catholic World* (November 5, 1945), p. 166.
13. *Saturday Review* (April 29, 1972), p. 27.
14. Ibid.
15. Wolcott Gibbs, *The New Yorker* (October 16, 1948), p. 51.
16. *Newsweek* (October 18, 1948), p. 88.
17. Kappo Phelan, *Commonweal* (October 29, 1948), p. 69.
18. The most vivid treatment of the minister's daughter was in the original short story that served as inspiration for *Summer and Smoke.* In "The Yellow Bird," Alma (Tutwiler) rebels more rigorously than her successors against the life of the rectory. Painting her face, dressing in loud colors, she quickly becomes the town's flashy bad girl, arriving home later and later from her downtown flings. When she surpasses the kind of excitement the small town can provide, she leaves, cavorting her way into the role of a legendary shady woman, giving birth to an illegitimate son, ending her days an old woman visited by her son who bears "fists full of gold and jewels that smelled of the sea." The story idealizes (and fantasizes) Alma's sexual transformation; she becomes the spirit of bohemian promiscuity. Alma's life is thus a kind of dream version of the Williams party world. For all its fanciful excess, though, the story has a flair and a mythic heightening that the plays aim for, but miss.·
19. *Saturday Review* (April 29, 1972), p. 27.
20. Ibid.
21. Irwin Shaw, *The New Republic* (December 22, 1947), p. 34.
22. *Saturday Review* (April 29, 1972), p. 27.
23. Joanne Stang, *New York Times* (March 28, 1965).
24. Elia Kazan, "Notebook for *Streetcar Named Desire,*" in *Directors on Directing,* edited by Toby Cole and Helen Krich Chinoy, p. 379.
25. Robert Brustein, "America's New Culture Hero," p. 125.

3. INTERLUDE

1. Joseph Wood Krutch complained that the play contains a sensible "hard core ... enveloped in a fuzzy haze of pretentious, sentimental, pseudo-poetic verbiage." (*The Nation*, April 14, 1945, p. 424.) Prophetically, Krutch anticipated the sort of criticism that has followed Williams throughout his career; critics complained of the playwright's predilection for effects, and his delight in lyrical verbal flights: "Probably he admires most in himself," wrote Krutch, "what is least admirable there. At the moment no doubt many agree with him. But they will not continue to do so for long. He is one of those writers who had best heed the advice: whenever you have written a line you like especially well, strike it out."
2. Mike Wallace, *New York Post* (December 30, 1957).
3. Stark Young, the best American critic of acting, praised the part of Amanda both as it was written and as it was played: "It is the best written role that I have seen in a play for years. All the language and the motifs are free and true; I recognized them inch by inch, and I should know, for I came from the same part of the country, the same locality and life, in fact, that Mr. Williams does.... Behind the Southern speech in the mother's part is the echo of great literature or at least a respect for it. There is the sense in it of her having been born out of a tradition, not out of a box. It has echo and the music of it.... Hers [Laurette Taylor's] is naturalistic acting of the most profound, spontaneous, unbroken continuity and moving life.... Technique, which is always composed of skill and instinct working together, is in this case so overlaid with warmth, tenderness and wit that any analysis is completely baffled." (*The New Republic*, April 16, 1945, p. 505.)
4. Edwina Dakin Williams, *Remember Me to Tom*, p. 149.
5. Ibid., p. 174.

4. DEPARTURES

1. Quoted by John Mason Brown, *Saturday Review* (March 10, 1951), p. 22.
2. Interview with Harry Gilroy, *New York Times* (January 5, 1951).
3. Harold Clurman, *The New Republic* (February 19, 1951), p. 22.
4. Interview with Gilroy.
5. Clurman, *The New Republic* (February 19, 1951), p. 22.
6. Walter Kerr, *Commonweal* (February 23, 1951), p. 493.
7. Brown, p. 22.
8. Euphemia van Renssalaer Wyatt, *Catholic World* (May 1953), p. 148.
9. Williams, quoted in Francis Donahue, *The Dramatic World of Tennessee Williams*, p. 58.
10. Harold Clurman, *The Nation* (April 4, 1953), p. 293.
11. Eric Bentley, *The New Republic* (March 30, 1953), pp. 30–31.
12. This passage was added for the published version.
13. Williams, quoted in John Gruen, *Close-Up* (New York, 1968), p. 91.

14. Williams, epilogue to published version of *Cat on a Hot Tin Roof* (Norfolk: New Directions, 1955).
15. Arthur B. Waters, "Tennessee Williams: Ten Years Later," p. 73.
16. Michael Mok, *New York World-Telegram and Sun* (November 17, 1960).
17. Marion Magid, "The Innocence of Tennessee Williams," p. 41.
18. Eric Bentley, *The New Republic* (April 11, 1955), p. 28.

5. THREE DARK PLAYS

1. *New York Times* (March 8, 1959).
2. Interview with Whitney Bolton, *New York Morning Telegraph* (January 26, 1959).
3. Tennessee Williams, "Five Fiery Ladies," *Life* (February 3, 1961), p. 88.
4. Arthur Ganz, "The Desperate Morality of Tennessee Williams," p. 290.
5. Harold Clurman, *The Nation* (January 25, 1958), p. 86.
6. Patrick Dennis, *The New Republic* (January 27, 1958), p. 20.
7. Kenneth Tynan, *The Observer* (September 2, 1958).
8. Quoted in Gilbert Maxwell, *Tennessee Williams and Friends,* p. 220.
9. Tynan.
10. Signi Falk, *Tennessee Williams,* p. 151.
11. Clurman.
12. Falk, p. 154.
13. Interview with Bolton.
14. Robert Brustein, "Williams's Nebulous Nightmare," *Hudson Review* (summer 1959), p. 255.
15. Kenneth Tynan, *The New Yorker* (March 21, 1959), p. 99.
16. John Hays, "Tennessee Williams's Use of Myth in *Sweet Bird of Youth,*" *Educational Theatre Journal* (fall 1966), p. 258.
17. Ibid.
18. Ganz, p. 294.
19. Brustein, p. 257.
20. Hays notes that worship of Adonis was "frequently accompanied by ritual castrations in imitation of Adonis' death—to insure the return of fertility in the spring... present mutilations offered up for greater harvests in the future..." p. 256.
21. Interview with *Theatre Arts* (January 1962), p. 19.

6. TWO "AFFIRMATIVE" PLAYS

1. Don Ross, *New York Herald Tribune* (November 6, 1960).
2. Arthur Gelb, *New York Times* (May 1, 1960).
3. Michael Mok, *New York World-Telegram and Sun* (November 17, 1960).
4. Interview with *Theatre Arts* (January 1962), p. 72.

5. Ross.

6. Interview with *Theatre Arts*, p. 72.

7. Seymour Peck, *New York Times* (December 24, 1961).

8. Harold Clurman, *The Nation* (January 27, 1962), p. 86.

9. Tennessee Williams, "A Summer of Discovery," *New York Herald Tribune* (January 3, 1962).

10. Williams, *New York Times Magazine* (October 29, 1961), p. 35.

11. Robert Brustein lamented the play's lack of narrative: "The author's compulsion to express himself on the subjects of fleshly corruption, time and old age, the malevolence of God, and the maiming of the sensitive by life has now become so strong that he no longer bothers to provide a substructure of action to support his vision. *The Night of the Iguana* enjoys no organizing principle whatsoever . . . very short on plot, pattern, or theme . . . while Williams has fully imagined his personae, he has not sufficiently conceived them in relation to one another, so that the movement of the work is backwards towards revelation of character rather than forwards towards significant conflict." *The New Republic* (January 22, 1962), p. 21.

12. Peck.

7. THE PLAYWRIGHT AS FAILURE

1. Harold Clurman, *The Nation* (June 2, 1969), p. 710.

2. Rex Reed, "Tennessee Williams Turns Sixty," *Esquire* (February 1972), p. 108.

3. Williams, in post-performance seminar at The New Theatre, New York, June 28, 1972.

4. Robert Brustein, *The New Republic* (February 15, 1963), p. 27.

5. Richard Gilman, *Commonweal* (February 8, 1963), p. 516.

6. Harold Clurman, *The Nation* (February 10, 1963), p. 106.

7. Williams, *New York Times* (August 25, 1963).

8. Interview with Don Ross, *New York Herald Tribune* (November 6, 1960).

9. Williams, *New York Times* (September 13, 1963).

10. Sam Zolotow, *New York Times* (November 27, 1963).

11. *Esquire* (August 1965), p. 95.

12. John Gruen, *Close-Up*, p. 93.

13. *Esquire* (August 1965), p. 95.

14. Harold Clurman, *The Nation* (March 14, 1966), p. 309.

15. Frances Herridge, *New York Post* (April 25, 1969).

16. Martin Gottfried, *Women's Wear Daily* (May 12, 1969).

17. Ibid.

18. Clive Barnes, *New York Times* (May 12, 1969).

19. John Simon, *New York* (May 26, 1969), p. 56.

20. Ross Wetzsteon, *The Village Voice* (May 22, 1969).

21. *New York Times* (June 10, 1969).

22. Charles Marowitz, *The Village Voice* (December 21, 1967).

8. DINGY BARS, FLEA-BAG HOTELS

1. Jim Gaines, "Interview with Tennessee Williams," p. 28.
2. Mel Gussow, *New York Times* (March 31, 1972).
3. Ibid.
4. Gaines, p. 28.
5. Henry Hewes, *Saturday Review* (April 22, 1972), p. 22.
6. Convinced that *Kingdom of Earth* sounded too much like "a Biblical drama," David Merrick renamed the play *Seven Descents of Myrtle*. Williams complained: "*Kingdom of Earth* is the title they bought . . . no one is going to tell me what my title should be. Theirs is vulgar." *New York Times* (February 21, 1968).
7. Williams, in fact, was working on an early draft of the play at the time of the production, in 1957, of *Orpheus Descending*. The original short story version (a wonderfully frank and lusty tale) was first published in a limited edition of *Hard Candy* in 1954.
8. Tennessee Williams, in conversation with William Burroughs, *The Village Voice* (May 16, 1977).
9. Ibid.
10. Interview with Mel Gussow, *New York Times* (July 15, 1975).
11. Williams continues to write. In 1977 and 1978, three new plays— *This Is (An Entertainment), Crève Coéur,* and *Tiger Tail,* a revision of *Baby Doll,* were produced by provincial companies.

BIBLIOGRAPHY

PLAYS

American Blues: Five Short Plays. New York: Dramatists Play Service, 1948.
Baby Doll and Two One-Act Plays. Norfolk, Connecticut: New Directions, 1956.
Camino Real. Norfolk: New Directions, 1953.
Cat on a Hot Tin Roof. Norfolk: New Directions, 1955.
Dragon Country: A Book of Eight Plays. New York: New Directions, 1970.
The Eccentricities of a Nightingale and *Summer and Smoke.* New York: New Directions, 1965.
The Glass Menagerie. New York: Random House, 1945.
In the Bar of a Tokyo Hotel. New York: Dramatists Play Service, 1969.
Kingdom of Earth (The Seven Descents of Myrtle). New York: New Directions, 1968.
The Milk Train Doesn't Stop Here Any More. New York: New Directions, 1964.
The Night of the Iguana. Norfolk: New Directions, 1962.
Orpheus Descending, with *Battle of Angels.* Norfolk: New Directions, 1958.
Period of Adjustment. Norfolk: New Directions, 1960.
The Rose Tattoo. Norfolk: New Directions, 1951.
A Streetcar Named Desire. Norfolk: New Directions, 1947.
Suddenly Last Summer. Norfolk: New Directions, 1958.
Sweet Bird of Youth. Norfolk: New Directions, 1959.
Twenty-Seven Wagons Full of Cotton and Other One-Act Plays. Norfolk: New Directions, 1946.
The Two-Character Play. New York: New Directions, 1969. (Signed limited edition.)
You Touched Me (with Donald Windham). New York: Samuel French, 1947.

SELECTED CRITICISM

Berkman, Leonard. "The Tragic Downfall of Blanche Du Bois." *Modern Drama* 10 (December 1967): 249–57.

Bluefarb, Sam. "The Glass Menagerie: Three Visions of Time." *College English* 24 (April 1961): 513–18.

Brooks, Charles. "The Comic Tennessee Williams." *Quarterly Journal of Speech* 44 (October 1958): 275–81.

Brustein, Robert. "America's New Culture Hero." *Commentary* 25 (February 1958): 123–29.

———. "Sweet Bird of Success." *Encounter* 12 (June 1959): 59–60.

Buckley, Tom. "Tennessee Williams Survives." *The Atlantic* 226 (November 1970): 98–108.

Donahue, Francis. *The Dramatic World of Tennessee Williams.* New York: Frederick Ungar, 1964.

Dukore, Bernard F. "The Cat Has Nine Lives." *TDR* 8 (Fall 1963): 95–100.

Falk, Signi. "The Profitable World of Tennessee Williams." *Modern Drama* 1 (December 1958): 172–80.

———. *Tennessee Williams.* New York: Twayne, 1961.

Fedder, Norman J. *The Influence of D. H. Lawrence on Tennessee Williams.* London, The Hague, Paris: Mouton & Co., 1966.

Gaines, Jim. Interview with Tennessee Williams. *Saturday Review* 55 (April 29, 1972): 25–29.

Ganz, Arthur. "The Desperate Morality of Tennessee Williams." *American Scholar* 31 (Fall 1962): 278–94.

Hurley, Paul J. "*Suddenly Last Summer* as a Morality Play." *Modern Drama* 8 (February 1966): 392–402.

———. "Tennessee Williams: The Playwright as Social Critic." *Theatre Annual* 21 (1964): 40–56.

Jackson, Esther. *The Broken World of Tennessee Williams.* Madison: University of Wisconsin Press, 1965.

Kazan, Elia. "Notebook for *A Streetcar Named Desire.*" *Directors on Directing,* edited by Toby Cole and Helen Krich Chinoy. New York: Bobbs-Merrill, 1963.

Keating, Edward M. "Mildew on the Old Magnolia." *Ramparts* 1 (March 1962): 69–74.

Lewis, R. C. "A Playwright Named Tennessee." *New York Times Magazine* (May 19, 1947), p. 19.

Magid, Marion. "The Innocence of Tennessee Williams." *Commentary* 25 (January 1963): 34–43.

Maxwell, Gilbert. *Tennessee Williams and Friends.* Cleveland and New York: World, 1965.

McCarthy, Mary. "A Streetcar Named Success," in *Mary McCarthy's Theatre Chronicles.* New York: Random House, 1954.

Nelson, Benjamin. *Tennessee Williams. His Life and Work.* New York: Astor-Honor, 1962.

Olley, Francis R. "Last Block on the Camino Real." *Drama Criticism* 8 (Fall 1965): 103–07.

Popkin, Henry. "The Plays of Tennessee Williams." *TDR* 4 (Fall 1960): 45–64.

Riddel, Joseph N. *"Streetcar Named Desire*—Nietzsche Descending." *Modern Drama* 5 (Winter 1963): 421–30.

Rogoff, Gordon. "The Restless Intelligence of Tennessee Williams." *TDR* 10 (Summer 1966): 78–92.

Roth, Robert. "Tennessee Williams in Search of a Form." *Chicago Review* 9 (Summer 1955): 86–94.

Sacksteder, William. "The Three *Cats:* A Study in Dramatic Structure." *Drama Survey* 5 (Winter 1966): 252–66.

Stanton, Stephen S. *Tennessee Williams. A Collection of Critical Essays.* Englewood Cliffs, New Jersey: Prentice-Hall, Inc., 1977.

Steen, Mike, ed. *A Look at Tennessee Williams.* New York: Hawthorn, 1969.

Tischler, Nancy. *Tennessee Williams: Rebellious Puritan.* New York: Citadel, 1961.

Vowles, Richard B. "Tennessee Williams and Strindberg." *Modern Drama* 1 (December 1958): 166–71.

Waters, Arthur B. "Tennessee Williams: Ten Years Later." *Theatre Arts Monthly* 39 (July 1955): 72–75.

Weales, Gerald. *Tennessee Williams.* Minneapolis: University of Minnesota Pamphlets 53 (1965).

Williams, Edwina Dakin. *Remember Me to Tom.* New York: Putnam's, 1963.

Williams, Tennessee. Introduction to *Reflections in a Golden Eye* by Carson McCullers. Norfolk: New Directions, 1950.

———. *Tennessee Williams' Letters to Donald Windham 1940-1965.* Edited with comments by Donald Windham. New York: Holt, Rinehart and Winston, 1977.

———. "A Writer's Quest for a Parnassus." *New York Times Magazine* (August 13, 1950), p. 16.

Yacowar, Maurice. *Tennessee Williams and Film.* New York: Frederick Ungar Publishing Co., 1977.

INDEX